WINNING

John D. A. Oakeley

WINNING
THE BOAT
THE CREW
& THE RACE

Adlard Coles
Erroll Bruce
Richard Creagh-Osborne

Nautical House
Lymington, Hampshire

Nautical Publishing Company

in association with George G. Harrap & Co. Ltd.,
London, Toronto, Sydney, Wellington

ISBN 0 245 51044 3

First published in Great Britain in 1970
NAUTICAL PUBLISHING COMPANY
Nautical House, Lymington, SO4 9BA, Hampshire

Second impression 1971
Second edition 1972

USA Edition 1971
French edition 1972
Italian edition 1972
Swedish edition 1972
German edition 1972
Japanese edition 1972

Composed in 12 on 13 pt Bembo (270)
and made and printed offset in Great Britain by
THE CAMELOT PRESS LIMITED
LONDON AND SOUTHAMPTON

Plate 1. John Oakeley and David Hunt sailing their world-champion Flying Dutchman *Shadow*

Plate 2. John Oakeley and his crew in his Soling *Surprise*. Note the small diameter mainsheet and spinnaker sheet, the novel boom section and the slide for the spinnaker boom at the base of the mast. Only essential items of equipment remain on deck. Everything else has been kept as low as possible, inside the boat.

FOREWORD

I first met John Oakeley five years ago in Holland when he was sailing the *Tempest* in the selection trials for a new IYRU two-man keel boat. *Tempest* was obviously the best boat but, just as obviously, she was also the best prepared and best sailed. We met again in Florida in 1966 when he won the keel-boat division in *Yachting*'s One of A Kind Regatta with another well-prepared, well-sailed *Tempest*. He simply did not make mistakes. All of which is not too surprising since John has won the Flying Dutchman world championship as well as numerous national or European championships in various dinghy classes. He has to be rated as one of the world's best small boat sailors.

I was therefore pleased to learn that John had written a book on yacht racing, pleased too when he asked if I would write the foreword. But I agreed to do so only if I felt the book offered a real contribution.

You already know the answer to that one because here I am writing the foreword! *Winning* is directed to the good sailor who wants to enter the big time, especially international races. The first part of the book, comprising a full seventeen chapters has to do with increasing boat speed. As John points out on the very first page, 'no matter how good the helmsman, the most brilliant tactics will look ridiculous if your boat is not moving fast through the water'. He goes into great depth concerning the preparation and the techniques to get your boat and you up to speed. If you're not a serious racing man, the amount of time and effort will appall you, may even convince you that you don't want to enter into major racing, in which case you can adapt what you care to in order to improve your performance for club racing. But if you aspire to compete with the very best, this Part I tells what you must do, and you had better believe it, despite the almost fanatical attention to detail John espouses. I can't imagine any keen sailor not picking up a number of useful pointers.

Part II deals with tactics and sailing techniques, and again it is written in relation to major racing. The author assumes you are already pretty good and then proceeds to tell you how you might become even better. It's all very sound and presents some new and stimulating thoughts.

When writing a book intended to make you an expert, it would seem all too easy for the author to appear stuffy or pontifical. John, however, is not only a very fine sailor but also a very nice and modest guy. The latter comes through loud and clear. He does not indulge in any false modesty, but he doesn't write down to the reader either. He merely tells you straight from the shoulder what you have to do to win in big time racing and tells it most clearly. Since you and I are not John Oakeley, he will doubtless keep right on beating us but if we have the fortitude and interest to do what he says, we should get better. And isn't that one of the goals of any racing man?

Thanks, John, for telling us all your secrets in such a clear and such a nice way.

Robert N. Bavier, Jr.
New York 1970

CONTENTS

LIST OF PLATES

ACKNOWLEDGEMENTS

Amongst the very many people who have helped me in writing this book, I would particularly like to thank the following:

John Gordon, who made most of the drawings.

My wife, Maureen, who typed out the tapes and re-typed the corrected script.

Ian Proctor Metals Masts Ltd. for their understanding and the loan of drawings.

And the following photographers and copyright-holders for giving the use of their pictures

Sports Illustrated	Charles Howard
Yachting World	W. W. Winter
Richard Creagh-Osborne	Bill Robinson
Frank Chapman	F.T.S.

PREFACE TO SECOND EDITION

The first edition of *Winning* was well received and has been translated into French, German, Swedish, Italian and Japanese as well as having a separate edition for the United States.

This new edition has been brought up to date where necessary and in particular has many new photographs. The continuing activity of the author in international events means that he is fully abreast of the latest techniques.

This work represents the considered opinions of a practical and successful racing skipper of very wide experience.

Lymington 1972

Part one:

the boat

1. The Hull

Planning your construction and layout—bare hull weight—light ends—deck layout—comfort—centreboard case—reducing windage on the hull

In this day and age it is virtually impossible to win major races with a standard boat; it is just the same in the car industry—you will not win races with a car straight out of the showroom, it has to be hotted up. Whether you are in the happy position of arranging to have the work done for you or whether, like most of us, you have to do the majority yourself, what has to be done remains the same. The boat must be taken to bits, adjusted, modified and put back together again with a finish that would put out of business any firm that tried to produce boats like it.

When planning international racing one has to team up with crew(s) with the intention of racing together for a certain period. In this way the boat can be moulded around the crew and the decks, toe straps, and everything adjusted to the crew's length and weight, etc. In a great many classes this is already done and you have only to go to the class championships and look at the different boats that are doing well to see that all the fittings have been adjusted differently to suit the individuals who sail them. You may think I am slighting the boat-builders for not turning out a boat of championship standard, but this is not so. Ten years ago one could buy any class boat from a leading boat-builder and go into a championship with a good chance of winning. Nowadays the pace is so hot that one just has to have that little bit of extra boat speed. No matter how good the helmsman, the most brilliant tactics will look ridiculous if your boat is not moving fast through the water.

When ordering a boat it is worth putting a great deal of prior thought into how you wish it built. Study past records of the class and check which builder has the most successes to his credit. One

thing is certain, his prices will be higher than anyone else's! If your
pocket won't stand it, try one of the others. I am sure they will be
only too willing to make a boat to your specification. If you win
with it they will be guaranteed a large slice of the market for the
next few years!

Minimum hull weight

Quite a number of boats built at the present time are built to
fishing-boat specifications—you should ask the builder to use the
minimum amount of material in building your boat. Merlin Rockets
and National Twelves are a good example, as the boat-builders tend
to use a much thicker planking than the minimum allowed by class
rules. Of course the boat-builder will argue that your boat will be
pounds under weight. This is a great advantage as it allows you to
put more weight in the middle of the boat. Class Rules give a maximum amount allowed for correctors of course, but on the other hand
this does not stop you from bringing the boat up to weight with a
lot of excess heavy fittings which, as the boat grows older and heavier,
can be removed one by one. This can usually be done quite legally
without having the boat re-measured as most rules state that only
correctors cannot be removed without re-measuring.

Light ends

With all the fittings in the middle of the boat the ends are very
light and this allows her to find the natural waterline when going to
windward or running downwind, although you may well have to
adjust it slightly to the crew's weight. I will cover this later.

When specifying that you want a light boat, it is advisable to ensure
that the mast gate, shroud attachments and centreboard case are
rigid and strongly built into the boat, as these are probably some of
the most highly stressed parts and will need careful attention.

Comfort must have priority!

The inside of the side decks, where allowed by class rules, should
be rounded and pads should be fitted into the inside of the hull to

accept toe straps. When Ian Proctor was designing the *Tempest*, he made up a paper model of me. It was complete with knee joints, and joints at shoulder and hip made with paper-clips. I presume that I was used for this model as I am of average build. When it was finished he designed the *Tempest* sidedecks, all internal layout and toe straps, etc., to fit my dimensions. The result was one of the most comfortable boats that I have had the pleasure to sail. One can sit out in *Tempest* for a great deal longer and without any of the numbness which is caused by sharp corners cutting the circulation. I think this is an ideal way to find the best deck layout and toe strap position.

Centreboard case construction

The centreboard case should be very carefully built, it must be absolutely vertical in the boat, its sides should not be warped and there should be no flexibility in the top. The latter can be achieved either by taking laminated struts from the top of the centreboard case out to the sides of the boat or by putting two very wide pieces of wood either side along the top. One end should be fastened to the thwart and the other to the inboard end of the toe straps' anchorage struts which should run out to meet the shroud fixing positions. In this way, when one is hard on the wind with the boat pulsing over the waves, there is no twisting at the top of the centreboard. The inside of the centreboard case can be lined with polytetrafluorethylene (P.T.F.E.), this is being used more and more in industry and boat-building, because it has a very low coefficient of friction, equivalent to wet ice on wet ice. If you cannot afford this, Formica or a similar hard smooth laminate can be used. This lining should only be on the forward half of the case and not in the after half where the centreboard does not rub. The side of the centreboard can also be lined with the same material, and this gives extra rigidity and it can still be hauled up and down with ease.

Position of shroud points

The shroud positions in the boat, in dinghies anyway, should be at least thirteen to fourteen inches aft of the mast. If you are using a large overlapping jib, as in the Dutchman class, set the shrouds in as

far from the outboard edge as possible. This would mean at least six
inches in the Dutchman.

Mast gate

Mast gates should allow the mast to move fore and aft only and
not athwartships. It is quite possible that at a later date you may
want clearance on each side of the mast, so one could design a mast
gate that not only had some sort of bend control fore and aft, but
also small adjustable chocks athwartships. This athwartships clearance
plays an important part in how the mast bends at spreader level.
Although it has not been tried yet I cannot help feeling that a certain
amount of side clearance here would be advantageous in light
weather.

Rubbing strake or gunwales

The rubbing strakes, if any are fitted, should be the maximum
allowed by class rules and only fitted at the position where the crew
and helmsman sit. For two reasons there should be none fore and aft
of this position—firstly to reduce the weight in the ends, and secondly
to allow the wind to flow smoothly over the hull without any
turbulence. One can argue that the rubbing strakes forward keep out
a great deal of water, but we now have such efficient bailers and
transom flaps that this argument is no longer valid.

The transom should be of the minimum depth, and should have
vent holes to allow wind to pass through it, thereby reducing the
turbulence on the after side when going to windward.

Spinnaker bag, chute, etc.

If your class allows spinnakers, you must try to fit yours into the
boat in the best possible position. The ideal is, without doubt, the
same as is used today in the Flying Dutchman class, i.e. a spinnaker
chute that emerges on deck just forward of the forestay. Unfortunately many classes do not allow this and a few still have the forestay
coming straight off the stem which makes this type of chute impossible
to fit. Keel boats often use spinnaker turtles, which are small bags

in which the spinnaker is folded and which are closed in with Velcro fastening strips. One good heave on the halyard rips open the Velcro fastener and allows the spinnaker to emerge. I think shortly we shall see a new era in hollow spinnaker booms where the spinnaker is fed inside rather like it is into the chute on the Dutchman. Although spinnaker stowage is a matter of personal preference, it is worth having a look at others in your class, find the most efficient and try to improve upon it. I have found that the majority of spinnaker bags have many rough edges. P.T.F.E. capping on these would allow the spinnaker to go up and down more easily.

What has been said already is also valid for keel boats, where again it is essential to have light ends, comfortable decks, and toe straps fitted in the right positions. This point will be quite a challenge in the Soling class, as this is the most uncomfortable boat to sit out that has ever been designed! I feel they will shortly be changing the rules on deck layout to enable the width of the deck to be reduced and slightly curved.

It would seem that with fibre glass boats which have fin keels there is a tendency for the keel to twist because the hull is sometimes not strong enough to withstand its stresses. It may be a wise precaution to insist upon extra stiffening at this point. It is of course extra weight but it is amidships and there is nothing worse than a keel that flaps about.

The underwater part of the hull should be as fair as possible, without sharp leading edges. I suggest the radius on all leading edges of keels should never be less than five millimetres whilst that on the rudder should be appreciably more.

Hull windage

Windage on all boats should be carefully considered. It is worth while removing the breakwaters where allowed, to take all the sheet leads, shroud attachments, spinnaker fittings, bow fairlead, in fact everything that is usually fitted above deck, below so that the wind can move over the hull with nothing to cause turbulence. It would seem from looking around the fleets of top class racing boats in the world today that nobody had ever heard of windage on the hull. I have seen bottlescrews on chain plates above deck taped up with the ends all unravelled and sticking out, compasses stuffed on deck with great domes sticking up, mast chocks with square edges projecting three-quarters of an inch above the deck and so on. Breakwaters seem to be the worst culprits. Goodness knows why they are still in fashion. In keel boats I have seen spinnaker poles stowed away on deck or up the mast, and contraptions fitted to trapeze wires to enable the crews to adjust the length. This combined with the handles they use for getting in and out flap around the leeward side of the boat in the slot of the jib and have a disastrous effect on the wind flow.

2. *Weight*

Weight distribution—bare hull weight—all-up sailing weight

If you were to ask me which type of weight I preferred, boat weight or crew weight I would answer every time, weight in the crew, as I consider weight in the boat is dead weight, i.e. weight that is fixed and cannot be used for trimming purposes, such as absorbing shocks, holding the boat upright and reducing the overall resistance of the boat to the water. With this in mind I think one should seriously tackle the problem of keeping the all-up weight of your boat down to a minimum. All-up weight is rarely taken into consideration, most people being interested in obtaining their new boats from the builders with minimum hull weight, and never considering the mast, boom, battens, sails, sheets and fittings that go into her afterwards. It goes without saying that for a start the bare hull should be well below minimum weight, and then brought up gradually, by painting the outside, varnishing the decks and inside, and then with the attachment of fittings.

Weight distribution

The position and weight of these fittings will have to be carefully studied to get them in the place for the most effective operation and also as low down in the boat as possible. If, before measuring, she is still underweight try putting lead keel bands on, making sure they are only positioned round the centreboard box, do NOT extend to the ends of the boat where it is better to change to aluminium or tufnol bands. Unless you are in the habit of running into other boats I cannot see any point in going to the top of the stem with the forward band; stop it at the forefoot.

All up sailing weight

Having acquired a boat which, with all the paint, fittings, etc., is down to bare hull weight, we must then start thinking again about the all-up weight, and this is the part that really matters.

I have been present at the weighing of numerous boats in the F.D. class and although the bare hull weight of these boats has always been down to within six to ten pounds of the minimum hull weight, there has been a difference of up to forty-five pounds in the all-up weight, mainly caused by an unfortunate choice of gear and excessive items of equipment the majority of which are never used!

In planning to get the all-up weight down a few points worth remembering are:

1. Keep the centreboard and rudder blade as strong and light as possible. The difference between a light and heavy centreboard can be as much as eleven or twelve pounds.
2. The rudder blade, rudder assembly, tiller and tiller extension are frequent culprits.
3. The mast should be the minimum weight allowed by class rules and special attention should be given to the boom and spinnaker boom.

Plate 3. Boom marks enable mainsail flow to be recorded and checked. The jib clew plate has different holes for the sheet connection to adjust the tensions on the leach and the foot of the jib. The gimballed compasses are by the aft handles on the deck but the spinnaker sheet often catches the compass and restricts the movement of the gimbals.

Plate 4. The little fluffy quarter-wave that all Tempests have when planing at this speed is clearly seen. Large diameter sheets for the main and spinnaker are not really necessary. Compare with photo 2. Remember that small sheets mean less weight. The transom holes connect with the cockpit to drain out surplus water.

4. The sails you cannot do much about except to make sure they are not made up of excessively heavy cloth.

5. All the cordage in the boat should be kept to a minimum. When choosing the type of rope that you intend using it is worth getting samples from different manufacturers, weighing them in a dry condition, and then leaving them in water for twenty-four hours. Weigh them again and you will see the extent of soakage that occurs. I find that in this respect sixteen-plait terylene rope is far superior to the eight-plait version.

6. In many classes the rigging is not calculated in the weight of the mast, and careful attention should be paid to the size of the wire and also the length. The majority of halyards on small keel boats and dinghies can be shortened by at least two or three feet. If everybody could be persuaded to bring halyards directly down on to the cleat rather than down through a sheave cage at the base of the mast and up, it would save at least half a pound and do away with the sheave cage.

7. Spreaders should be carefully studied, they must be made up of aluminium and not of stainless steel. To get the necessary strength they may well have to be of an aerofoil section.

8. Paddles should be left ashore, unless the class rules state otherwise, if so they should be very small and light.

9. Anchors would naturally be down to the minimum weight, but why bother to carry an anchor line. Once the mainsail and jib are up and the wire on the halyard attached directly to some hook or tension lever there is no reason why the tail rope of the halyards should not be removed, joined together and used as the anchor line. This will keep the base of the mast neat and solves the problem of the additional weight of an anchor line.

10. A careful check on the battens should be made, it may be possible to make them lighter by using a different type of wood or even to thin them down.

11. All shackles should be carefully checked to see whether smaller ones can be used.

12. If you are using winches, are they the lightest on the market?

13. What about the mainsheet blocks, spinnaker blocks, etc., are there lighter ones available?

14. Bottlescrews, get rid of them and use link plates.

15. Can the weight of your spinnaker bags be reduced?
16. Are there small bits and pieces from previous years which are not now used that can be removed?
17. Keep the bailer and sponge up underneath the deck where they can stay dry (if you are wondering why, try weighing a wet sponge).
18. Have some means of keeping your spinnaker dry, not only is a wet spinnaker hard to haul up but think of its weight!
19. What about the burgee, small and light?

I hope that these points may help as a check list on your own boat. If you really go to town on all the points mentioned you may well reduce the all-up weight considerably. Try weighing the boat before you start and then with all the items of gear you would use if going afloat. To show you to what lengths some people will go to reduce weight in the boat, Mario Capio of Italy drilled out the centres of all the bolts holding fittings on his Flying Dutchman, and not content with that he proceeded to put four or five holes in each of the nuts! You may well say this is going too far but . . .!

3. Hull Finish

Paint—varnish—outside of hull—deck—inside of hull—water adhesion to deck surface—centreboard and rudder

Much has been written about the application of paint and varnish. The number of coats needed and the type of primers to use. I do not think it necessary to go into it all again in this book. The make of paint and varnish used is entirely a personal matter and I am sure that the leading manufacturers products are all equally good. But there is one type of paint and varnish I find ideal on a racing hull and that is the two-pack polyurethane. If used in accordance with the maker's instructions and mixed well it lasts indefinitely with the minimum amount of upkeep. It would appear from my experience of using polyurethane that it should be used mainly on boats that are dry sailed. It does have a tendency, because it is so hard, for water to creep in the back of it and be unable to get out again. It causes the paint to lift, whereas with the ordinary type of paint, with a greater porosity, the water can get out again through the paint, so keeping a more balanced moisture content.

Hull finish

Polyurethane paint on the outside of the hull cut back with four hundred grade wet-and-dry, and polished with a very fine grinding paste, gives a surface second to none. There is a product on the market called 'Graphite' paint. The makers claim that this paint has less surface friction, but my experience is that if it has, it is too small to be noticeable. However, Graphite paint properly applied, and rubbed down with six hundred grade wet-and-dry gives a beautiful finish for very little work. One disadvantage is that while doing it you will tend to look like an old-fashioned chimney sweep!

I personally think the hull should be of one colour and never have different coloured topsides and bottom since this must always leave a join mark where the two colours meet, and this is doubled if you use a boot topping. No matter how hard you try you will never be able to get rid of these ridges completely.

The minimum number of coats on the outside should be nine. These should be rubbed down well so that the thickness of paint is not too great and the weight kept down. I find an orbital sander ideally suited for this as it rapidly removes all high spots and jumps over the low ones, making a much fairer hull.

If you have any pet theories regarding one type of paint or another allowing less skin friction, then make sure the whole boat is painted with it and not just the bottom. It amuses me to see the Ocean and Off-shore Racers spending enormous sums of money equipping themselves and getting a marvellous finish below the water but forgetting that one topside or the other is fully immersed at least fifty per cent of the sailing time!

Deck finish

The deck should be treated rather like the outside of the hull, but with six coats of paint only as this part of the boat is very easy to rub down to give another coat at any time it is needed. It does not need to have a perfect finish in fact, on keel boats, I find that non-slip deck paint is hard to beat, especially if applied to fibre glass upperworks. Admittedly it wears off after a while, but again it is very easy to apply an extra coat. Before rubbing down to paint or varnish do not forget to remove any fittings since excessive build up around the bases can be a time wasting factor later when they have to be removed.

Internal finish

The inside of a boat always gets a battering, and the working area where the crew and helmsman stand should have at least nine coats, but there is no need to give the inside at each end of the boat, underneath the fore and aft decks, any more than four. After all, paint or varnish here is only used to keep the water out, and the last thing you want is excessive weight in these areas. I do not think a good finish is necessary on the inside. After rubbing down I always brush out as much dust as I can and what is left is brushed in with the varnish. It goes towards making a non-slip surface! Underneath the sidedecks will need at least two coats and so either turn the boat upside down on trestles and use a brush or get hold of a spray gun for the job. I find a gun much better and quicker, it gets in all the nooks and crannies so stopping any water getting into the deck.

The transom can be varnished if you prefer it. Very little of its surface comes in contact with the water and the number of coats should also be kept to a minimum as it is at the extreme end of the boat where lightness is most important.

Skin friction

There has been much talk about polymers and various types of polishes for the outside of the hull; some of these have been banned and others have been proved useless. Any type of wax polish is of course, useless. If you want to experiment with surface finishes you could follow Charles Currey's example. When he was at the top of the International Fourteen fleet, before a Prince of Wales Cup race, he rolled his boat over and covered the underwater surface with the white of an egg. This he let harden in the sun, waited until the last minute to launch, and rushed out to the start. Of course as soon as the boat entered the water the egg white started to dissolve. Charles never did tell me if he won the race!

There is a theory that air bubbles reduce skin friction and I rather believe this is true. I have felt many times that there has been an increase in speed when I have opened the self bailers and after the water has been drained out the self bailer has been left sucking down air. This air presumably, on leaving the self bailer, spreads out over the part of the hull. Because of this mass of bubbles running along the hull it is acting rather like a continuous stream of ball-bearings separating the hull from the water.

I understand the Americans were experimenting with this theory some time ago by having a pipe running round the hull just forward of the mast. This pipe had many very small holes drilled in it so that air, being fed in under pressure, was forced out through the holes giving off masses of air bubbles that were swept aft over the hull by the movement of the water. I think this experiment came to an end when it was found that polymers pumped into the same tube produced a better result.

Water adhesion

I have often worried about the amount of water that has splashed on to the deck while sailing, which does not run off because it sticks on to the varnished surface. An experiment will show you just how serious this problem is—when you have newly varnished your deck, get a hose and spray water all over the boat, or just leave it out in the rain, you can then sponge off the globules of water that are left lying there and then squeeze it all into a bucket. You will be surprised at the amount there is. With my Dutchman I squeezed off three-quarters of a bucketful which weighed approximately seven pounds.

This is an unnecessary handicap to carry around during a race and every effort should be made to get over this problem. One way is to rub the deck down very gently with six hundred grade wet-and-dry paper and the water then runs away almost completely, and so it would seem that the globules will only sit around on a shiny surface. This is also a problem the Admiralty are trying to solve, since they have great troubles with the amount of water that accumulates on the sides and superstructure of destroyers and other small warships. This is aggravated by the fact that there are rivet heads and other projections which stop the water running away. There have been many experiments with different types of paint but at the present time no solution has been found.

The centreboard and rudder blade I have left until last as I consider these to be the most important underwater parts of the boat. It goes without saying that the equivalents in a keel boat, which are the fin keel and rudder blade, are equally important and can be treated in the same way.

Centreboard and rudder

The centreboard and rudder both work under pressure from the water either one side or the other and therefore the surface of these two must be even more perfect than surfaces operating at a lower pressure. It is generally understood that a surface which has a stream of water forced upon it under pressure, will offer far more resistance than a surface operating at a lower pressure. As far as I know the only way to get the finish needed is hard work and elbow grease! All the hollows must be cemented up and at least nine coats of paint applied. When these nine coats have cured and hardened the surface should then be rubbed down to the bare wood using two hundred grade wet-and-dry paper wrapped around a block of wood. This is the first time I have mentioned using a block with wet-and-dry, which has the effect of bridging the larger but gentler undulations you may have missed when cementing. Having rubbed down to the bare wood, or as near as possible, another four coats of paint should be applied. When this has hardened and cured it should be rubbed down with four hundred to six hundred grade wet-and-dry paper, without the block. On rubbing this down for some time you will find the paint will eventually start to go transparent. When this happens give one last rub down lubricated with soft soap, or you can use ordinary household detergent if it is nice and thick. After this wash the surface thoroughly and leave to dry. When quite dry rub down with a metal polish, such as 'Bluebell', using a very dry rag.

This will all take some considerable time but the final finish will be a just reward for all your time and effort.

It is worth remembering that centreboards and rudder blades should either be varnished or painted white—never coloured. A board painted black will warp immediately if it is left in the slightest sunshine owing to heat absorption, and it is doubtful if you will ever get it to go back into shape again. It is worth having two centre boards and two rudder blades, one pair for really important races and the other for normal club racing where it is not so disastrous if you run aground or chip the ends. On this pair you can always fill up the chips with cement and they can be finished off properly at some other time.

4. Fittings

Requirements—positioning—weight—centre mainsheet arrangements—toe straps

At any major regatta you should spend many hours inspecting the other competitors' boats to see just what fittings they have and how they are positioned. While you are doing this the other skippers will be looking at your boat. Finding out how competitors from other countries tackle the same problems is one of the most interesting aspects of international sailing.

I am now going to try to go through all the fittings that are used on dinghies and small keel boats and discuss the different types that are available, the positioning of these fittings, and probably most important of all, how to use these fittings correctly. I will, without doubt, miss a few and many of you will not agree with my reasoning. But surely half the fun of sailing is being an individualist and creating fittings to suit one's own requirements.

When setting out to buy fittings for your boat go through several different manufacturers' catalogues and find out what is available and compare the items. The sort of things to look for are minimum and maximum size, minimum weight, good fixing points, smooth running and no sharp edges. Beware of anything containing a variety of materials which may wear unevenly or become unworkable due to electrolysis. Beware also of anything with nylon incorporated in it if the fitting is to be used under high stress loads such as for shrouds and jib sheets. Nylon is also bad for such things as bullseyes which may have rope running through them at high speeds. Heat is generated which softens the nylon. The rope or wire then cuts through the nylon which jams it.

Make sure you use the correct size of shackle for the job and, most important, make sure the shackle is of stainless steel.

Fittings for adjustment purposes

Where fittings are required for adjustment purposes they must have positive stops so that there is no chance of slipping while in use. It is also of great advantage to have some sort of vernier adjustment so that very fine alterations can be made.

Winches

Reel winches and drum winches are not good for fine adjustment since, when under tension, the wire tends to slip round the spindle and also, when winding up, if the wire overlaps one of the turns already on the spindle, it takes up approximately half as much again as it did on the first turn. Also the drum winches are controlled by a length of small line which can stretch under tension.

For highly stressed fittings avoid castings unless X-rayed, since it is easy for them to have air holes at points of critical stress and which are concealed from visual inspection.

Self bailers

Self bailers should be of the 'wedge' type and not of the 'tube' or 'probe' type. Although this 'probe' works well it does create resistance to the water flow over the hull, it picks up weed, and if you hit anything it will distort and you will not be able to pull it up. Probably the most efficient self bailers on the market today are the Elvström

Figure 1. One of the five models of Elvström bailer.

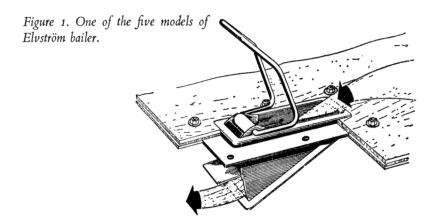

types which, although very expensive, are well worth the money (Figure 1). A cheaper version which is nearly as efficient is the Jack Holt plastic model which initially had many teething troubles but they seem to have been solved now.

Stemhead fittings

The stemhead fittings vary on different boats. Some classes allow jib furling gear, others prohibit it, while boats like the Flying Dutchman, Fireball and Soling, have their jib tack and forestay set well aft of the stemhead and need a completely different method of fixing altogether.

Starting with the stemhead fittings, if the class allows you to sail without a forestay, then do not have any fitting here at all. Drill a hole through the deck and take a tack strop wire down through the top of the stem to a sheave just below and back either to some means of adjustment, or even fix it on to the hog or backbone. This will allow you to get your jib tack as low as possible and also avoid any heavy fittings that may project up above the deck. You can put a small fairing piece of tufnol where the wire goes through the deck to stop chafe.

If a furling gear is allowed there are many good types on the market of which, probably the best known is the 'Tradewind' model. This can be let into the top of the stemhead and the jib tack can be attached directly on to it.

If the class rules say that a forestay must be fitted, then this makes life a little difficult and you have a choice of two positions for the forestay. One is for it to be far enough forward to clear the jib luff when furling, and the other is to attach it directly to the top of the furling gear in which case, if your jib has a very small diagonal measurement, you can roll up the forestay as well as the halyard. Incidentally if you do have such a narrow footed jib there is no real need to have 'a swivel for the top of the halyard as the number of turns necessary to wind up the jib can easily be taken up by twisting the wire halyard.

With boats that are allowed forestays and jib tacks set inboard and are allowed holes in the deck, it is possible to fit a spinnaker chute. It appears that the spinnaker chute was first thought up by Roberts of America approximately six years ago. To start off it was not a great success, but eventually it was perfected and is now an essential part of the boat equipment. Spinnaker chutes may be obtained from most leading boat-builders and are easily fitted. The technique of using a spinnaker with a chute will be dealt with later in the book.

Jib cunningham hole

More and more people are using a cunningham hole on the jib luff. I personally do not really believe the use of this is generally understood, but I think that by the time this book is published a definite technique will have been established. I think the best way to rig the cunningham hole is to have a very light wire strop running from the hole in the tack of the jib, down through a sheave in the deck and back to a two or three part purchase underneath the deck or somewhere else in the boat. The final part can come back to either the crew or the helmsman, whichever is preferred.

It is not possible to have a separate wire if one is using a furling gear. In this case the wire has to go down a tube which forms the central part of the furling gear to a swivel situated in the base of this shaft. From then on the wire passes round a sheave at the base of the gear and then back to the purchase again. Various manufacturers make this, the best known is the Sea Sure model.

Shroud attachments

Shroud attachment points are some of the most important parts of the boat:

1. They must be strong enough;
2. They must be in the correct position;
3. They must have the correct means of adjustment.

To take the first point, the boat should always be reinforced in the area of the shroud attachments either by having extra layers in the skin or by a knee or pad under the deck. When fitting the shrouds onto the hull of the boat it is essential that all fastenings are in shear and not in tension. Huge strains are imposed upon this fitting when running in heavy weather. If such fastenings have to be in tension then the number of these fastenings should be doubled. It makes a difference to the strength of the attachment points if the shroud is lined up correctly with the fitting rather than twisting it (see Figure 2).

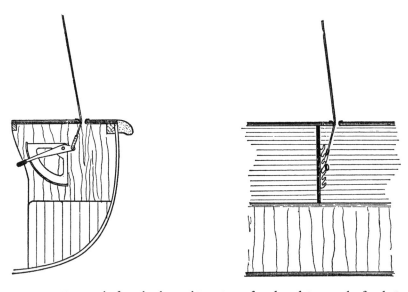

Figure 2. Fore-and-aft and athwartships view of a shroud incorrectly fitted. It should have been arranged to line up with the lever.

The type of fitting used for adjusting the tension on the stays is a matter of personal preference. Again there are many types on the market. The simplest is the vernier rack in which, as you can see from Figure 3, the stay end is attached to a strip of metal with a series of holes drilled at a set pitch. This strip of metal slides within a folded 'U' section piece of stainless steel which is attached to the hull and which also has a series of holes drilled through it but at a slightly different pitch. It is then possible to have as little as two millimetres of adjustment simply by putting the locking pin into a different hole.

The stay or shroud lever, see Figure 4, is at present used only for centreboard boats. This is probably the most satisfactory means of adjusting the stay since it can be operated very quickly while underway. You can also easily remember where the lever is set

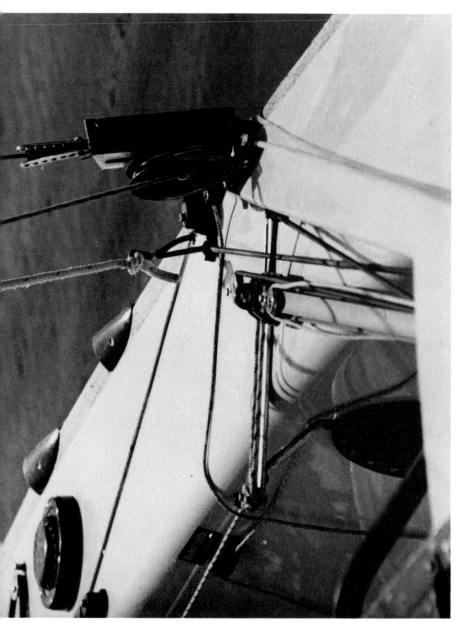

Plate 5. An interesting shroud-tensioning device. The shroud is attached to a sheave inside the box. A wire from the bottom of the box runs up and over the sheave and down to the spindle of the drum winch. This method gives ample purchase and is quick, simple and very light.

Plate 6. Hydraulic shroud tensioner. By inserting a handle in the top end of the pump it is possible to exert great pressures with minimum effort. Problems appear to be its weight and its vulnerability to damage in a collision.

Figure 3

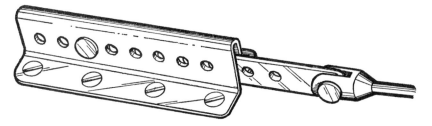

so that you can always get it back into the same place after taking the tension off.

For the initial adjustment there is a small link plate at the top of the lever, which can be arranged as a vernier if needed, so that you can get the tensions on opposite stays exactly the same for the same position of lever.

Another adjusting device, which has been developed by Sea Sure is like one half of a rigging screw, with a big wheel on the male part. This is good, although it once suffered from the fact that registering the position of the adjustment was too imprecise; this has since been rectified. One side of the screw thread has been ground away leaving a flat on which they have marked a very easily read scale, but the adjustment is still not as quick to use as the lever.

Figure 4

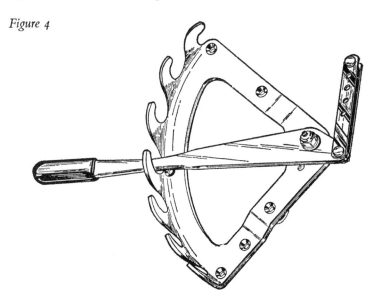

If you arrange to have the stay attachments fastened to the boat in the normal position it is possible only for the crew to alter them. It may be essential for the helmsman to be able to adjust the stays while the crew is up on the foredeck, looking after the spinnaker or out on the trapeze, in which case, it is possible to lead the stays back aft to any one of these fittings within easy reach of the helmsman. If this is done you will need to fit a very robust sheave cage under the deck for the shroud wire. A word of warning here, nowhere in this sheave cage must nylon or tufnol be used. It must be made entirely from either bronze or stainless steel. It is probably best and most convenient to have flexible wire running round the sheave cage which is then fastened on to the main stay via a rigging link. On no account use shackles—in fact shackles should not be used anywhere in the standing rigging system—only stainless steel links and pins should be used.

Jib fairleads

Jib fairleads whenever possible should be positioned below deck level. This may well mean cutting a slot in the deck, but I do not think that this matters when one considers the advantage one gains through not having a bulky fairlead and rope above the deck causing wind disturbance.

There are so many different types of fairlead on the market that I could not mention all of them and so I will concentrate on the latest models. Unfortunately those that are readily available on the market do not always lend themselves to being positioned below the deck and so, for this reason, choose carefully.

I will start with those that can be positioned only on deck. The ratchet fairlead manufactured by Beta Marine is one of the latest additions to the fairlead range and is exceedingly good, although not at present manufactured on a track for adjustment in the fore-and-aft direction. It is too small to use as a fairlead for small keel boats, but could be quite useful as a spinnaker fairlead. The ratchet on the wheel of the fairlead allows the rope to come in easily but will not revolve the other way and so the rope has to run over a grooved sheave which creates much resistance.

The ratchet fairlead is similar in many ways to the Lewmar 'Novex' block which I consider to be one of the greatest aids to racing dinghies since bendy masts. This block is cleverly designed so that the ratchet gear which controls the rotation of the sheave only engages when a set amount of tension comes on to the rope. If and when the wind drops light and the weight on the rope becomes less, or if the hauling part is let go, the ratchet gear in the sheave disengages and allows the pulley to rotate as a standard block. The person holding the hauling part of the rope is able to control a very high loading for a great length of time without getting tired. This really makes it ideal for jib sheets and also the spinnaker and main sheets.

Many manufacturers have tried to copy this idea, but none has succeeded in producing a block which is smaller and does the job as effectively. For use as jib fairleads these Novex blocks can be fastened to a track by means of a shackle on a slide, in which case they are free to take their own line between the crew's hand and the jib clew. This simple method of mounting does allow the position of the jib fairlead to move about somewhat, but a bracket can be obtained so that the block is lying flat on a back plate which attaches to the track. This is much better as it has a positive fixing so that you can mark and note the position of your fairleads. Another advantage with this block is that it can be attached to a track below deck level and because it can be made to swivel and rotate it is possible for it to take up the correct line between the jib clew and the crew position wherever he may be situated.

A fitting made by M. S. Gibb consists of a tufnol bullseye on twin tracks and it is ideally suited if you want to have your sheets on top of the deck. The main advantage of this fairlead is that it is possible to position it anywhere within the boundaries of the track either forward or athwartships by a very simple means of adjustment. There are many other makes of fairlead on the market which are usually made of nylon, wood or tufnol of the bullseye type either with or without tracks. I do not feel that these are really suitable for sheeting sails on out-and-out racing boats although they are ideally suited for small cruising dinghies.

Barber hauler

If you mount your jib fairlead on the deck or running through the deck, close to the clew of the jib, for example, with less than eighteen inches (457 mm.) between the deck and the clew you are going to need what is called a 'Barber hauler'. How this name came about I do not know, but I gather it originated in the United States and it is not really a fitting but a method.

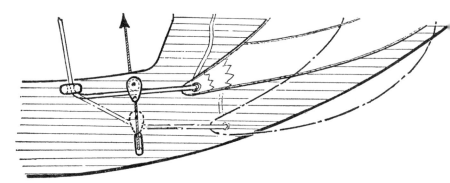

Figure 5. The barber-hauler block is used to pull the jib clew further outboard.

When one is sailing to windward one needs the fairleads inboard and quite well aft. The trouble with this is that although it is fine when going to windward the position is useless once you ease the jib sheet for a reach, since the clew of the jib is pulled back towards the centreline again and the top of the jib sags off. This fellow, Barber, who ever he may be, invented a method whereby he had the jib sheets running through a small light block between the clew and the fairlead. This block was attached to a short length of line that ran through a bullseye or sheave situated just inside the gunwale some distance forward of the normal fairlead. When the sheet was eased on a reach Mr. Barber then tightened up on his rope, which had been led across the boat to the windward side into a jam cleat. By tightening this rope he was able to pull the block on the bight of the jib sheet outboard and forward thereby giving a much better lead to the jib sheet. This method of sheeting on a reach is becoming universal. I have tried it myself and find it good, but don't do what I did the first couple of times and forget to let go. I could not understand why I was unable to point high! (Figure 5.)

Plate 7. An idea for a Dragon is this use of a re-circulating ball mainsheet traveller for attaching the genoa sheet block. This enables easy adjustment of the athwartships position of the genoa clew, i.e. bringing it inboard in light weather and letting it out when it blows hard.

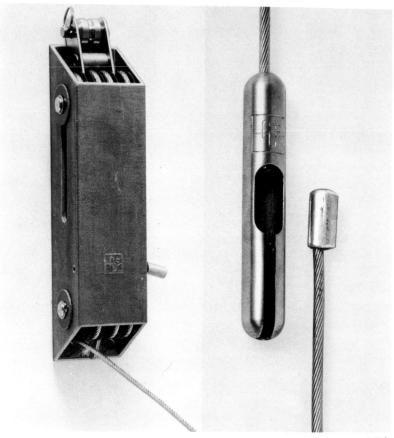

Plates 8 and 9. On the left is an eight-part wire purchase which can be used for adjusting shrouds while under tension or for any other adjustment under heavy loading.

On the right is a neat fitting which will pass up the interior of a hollow mast, and allow the tail of a halyard to be detached after the sail is hoisted so that it can be stowed or otherwise used. It can be used for rope or wire.

Mast bend control

Years ago, before bendy masts came into popular use the mast could be either stepped in an inkpot on top of the deck, or it was stepped on the keel and fitted snugly into a slot at deck level. Nowadays, when it is essential to have a bendy mast, one must have some means of controlling this bend. Unfortunately mast bend control devices have not advanced quite as quickly as have other items of equipment and there is a big gap in the market just waiting for someone to produce a fitting that is suitable for the majority of dinghies and small keel boats.

At the present time there are three models of bend control device on the market and many quite good fittings are being made by owners for their own boats. The first of the trade fittings that appeared was designed by Lanaverre of France and consisted of an alloy arm pivoted near one end. The short end had a large roller fitted to it which pressed up against the forward face of the mast and by pulling on the long end of the arm it was possible to apply considerable pressure to the front of the mast via the roller. It worked well, but unfortunately does not fit the majority of classes although is ideally suited for the Five-O-five and in some cases, the Dutchman (Figure 6).

Figure 6. The lever and roller method of limiting forward bend at deck level.

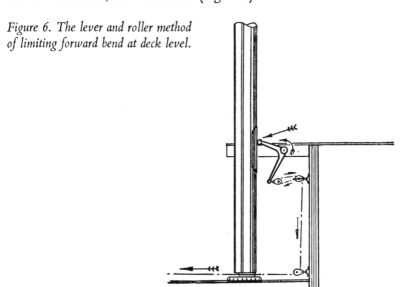

Then came the device thought up by Cliff Norbury for his *Tempest* which consists of a length of channel with a plunger in the middle, one end of which was connected to a drum-type winch. When tension was applied to the winch, pressure was exerted on the plunger which was then transmitted to the front face of the mast (see Plate 16). Another type using a rack and pinion is shown in Plate 15.

Probably the simplest and easiest to fit is the one thought up by Kurt Bier of F.T.S. in Germany. This is a small alloy box with a plunger inside and a six-to-one purchase attached to the plunger. By pulling on the end of the line considerable force is produced against the front of the mast.

You will notice that of the four I have described above none gives an absolute and positive lock, nor can they be graduated accurately so that you can record the position at which you lock the mast. The best I have yet seen that does both these things was made up by John Truett for his *Dutchman* (see Plate 14). This is small, simple, and registers the fore-and-aft position of the mast, and will not move until adjusted. So far this fitting has not been manufactured commercially and so I suggest you make it up yourself.

If you find you cannot obtain any of these fittings, or that if they are on the market, they will not fit your boat and you have not the time to make one up for yourself, I suggest you use what I have used for the last four or five years, that is, ordinary wooden mast chocks of various thicknesses, each numbered. It is just a matter of removing one or other of the chocks to get the right amount of bend. It may not be the ideal solution but it is certainly the cheapest!

Centre mainsheet traveller

Centre mainsheets have been tried on and off for many years but it was not until the middle nineteen-fifties that Ken Rose brought out a beautifully engineered, radiused, tufnol track with a traveller made up from rollers. It seemed to work very well, the only snag being that it tended to be a little cumbersome. The idea of this radiused track, which incidentally went from gunwale to gunwale, was to do away completely with the kicking strap, and if my memory serves me correctly, he had a fixed mainsheet, i.e. just a single part on a drum winch rather like a kicking strap so that, when sailing, all he then had to do was to adjust the traveller position. I always felt his boat went well with this set up and he walked away with his first race at Hamble, but unfortunately he did not persevere with it and he eventually sold the boat.

After that it was a long while before anyone tried again. I think the main reason that centre sheeting did not catch on was that it was very difficult to devise an efficient system for allowing the bottom end of the main sheet to run in and out, which tended to put people off. Unless they spent a great deal of money on the design and engineering of the mainsheet slide they had to have a standard sail track strapped across their thwart with an ordinary slide on it. In the majority of cases this ended in frequent capsizes and so gradually everybody transferred back to the transom mainsheet system.

My view now is that even if they had at that time had the centre mainsheet attachment point on the boat fixed on the centreline it would still have been much better than the sliding transom mainsheet. It was not until the early nineteen-sixties when Ian Proctor Metal Masts brought out their recirculating ball-bearing traveller, that centre mainsheets could become a practical proposition. I think that from this time there has been a steady transfer to the centre mainsheet arrangement.

The mainsheet traveller designed by Proctors was unique in the fact that it could take any type of loading, i.e. compression, tension, twisting, without ever jamming. It was a very long time before any other manufacturer brought on to the market anything to compare with it.

There is still of course the mainsheet slider introduced in the Finn class which consisted of a piece of tube fixed at either end with a slide or skate running across it, but this is not particularly satisfactory as the skate only works in tension and also the bar that goes across, if put into a boat with a wider span than has the Finn, tends to bend too much unless it is very strong and heavy.

Two or three years after Proctor introduced the recirculating ball-bearing traveller the demand for travellers increased so much that other manufacturers were persuaded to produce their own. From then on we have had an influx of different types, all quite good and many cheaper than the original Proctor model.

When using a centre mainsheet, the final part of the purchase should be taken down to the bottom of the boat through a swivel block. My strong recommendation for this block is a Novex because when reaching I find that if one has adjusted the position of the traveller, to suit the point of sailing, it is worth playing the mainsheet, and although this can be done directly through a standard block it is too tiring to do so for any length of time and a Novex is therefore essential.

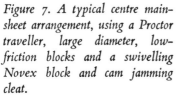

Figure 7. A typical centre mainsheet arrangement, using a Proctor traveller, large diameter, low-friction blocks and a swivelling Novex block and cam jamming cleat.

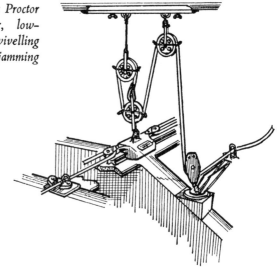

Centre mainsheet jammer

There are various means of jamming the mainsheet. One of the commonest is to jam it on the weather side deck after it has come through the block. This has certain limitations, especially when tacking when it means that you must uncleat the mainsheet, go about, and then cleat up on the other side. This is fine if you have three arms so that you can adjust the traveller at the same time! In my boat I designed a swivelling jam cleat on to which was attached a Novex block, in this way I was able to jam the mainsheet in the centre of the boat and then play the mainsheet traveller whilst going to windward and when going about without ever having to adjust the mainsheet. The cleat was always there at my feet ready for releasing or tightening whichever direction I was facing. Sad to say, centre mainsheet jammers that will accept Novex blocks are not yet manufactured and once again it seems to be just a question of waiting for some enterprising manufacturer to come up with a fitting at a reasonable price.

You can see in the drawing the type of fitting I used in conjunction with a mainsheet traveller. This fitting swivels on the centre base, and has a Novex block attached to a pair of jaws, which keep the block upright. There is also a loop on the after side of the cam jammer to make the whole fitting swivel towards you when you pull the loose end of the mainsheet.

The position of this fitting is quite critical. It should be as low as possible in the boat to give enough distance between it and the boom so that the mainsheet traveller can go virtually to the end of its track.

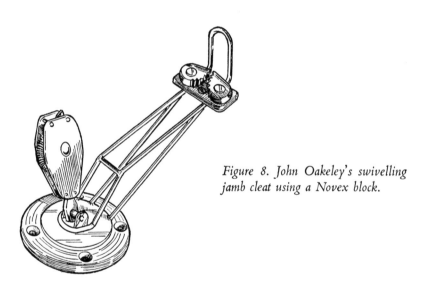

Figure 8. John Oakeley's swivelling jamb cleat using a Novex block.

Traveller control lines

The control lines for the traveller should be simple and easy to use and I would suggest that there should be a two-part purchase using a single block on the traveller with one end of the line fixed on the sidedeck and the other passing back through a fairlead somewhere near the end of the track, and then through a jamming cleat with a fairlead which is placed easily to hand. The rope needs to be thicker than one might think and I suggest one and a quarter inch circ. (12 mm. dia.). This large size is to stop the rope cutting your hands to ribbons, since the traveller has to be used constantly when going to windward. One can reduce the tension by putting in more purchase, but this reduces the speed with which you can play the traveller and therefore I think it is not practical.

Transom mainsheet

If you have a transom mainsheet it is worth while, if the class rules allow, to have a full length mainsheet track, but this does not have to be of the expensive roller type. It need only be a piece of sail track with slides and a couple of adjustable stops on it. The final lead of the mainsheet can then be taken through a Novex block. This system works well, especially if you put adjusting lines on to the end stops, and cross them over so that the leeward one is adjustable from the windward side.

One point to remember, with the transom mainsheet is that the boom must project beyond the transom. A rather nice luxury is to have the boom projecting by approximately twelve inches (30 cms.) and to fix a small track underneath the outboard end of the boom, to which can be fastened a small sliding eye. The position of this eye can then be adjusted according to how much compression you wish to place on the gooseneck, to bend the mast (see Figure 9).

Spinnaker sheet leads

Spinnaker sheets, whenever possible, should be led through large diameter low-friction sheave cages which, incidentally, you will have to make yourself as there are none on the market as yet. These should be positioned as far aft as possible, except for use with a short-footed spinnaker, when it is advisable to bring forward the position of the sheave cage so that the spinnaker sheets are at the right angle. Otherwise there will not be enough downward pull on the spinnaker sheet, and the clew of the spinnaker will be too high, therefore upsetting the balance of the whole sail. On keel boats one can fit a spinnaker sheet retainer. This is a very light line running from a small block

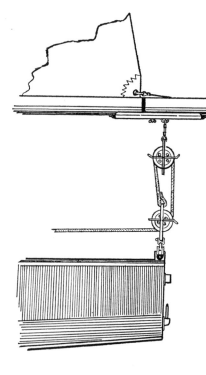

Figure 9. A transom sheeting system with a slide on the under side of the boom, so that the pressure on the gooseneck at the mast can be varied.

sliding on the spinnaker sheet, through a fairlead on the gunwale, or better still through a bullseye in the deck to a jam cleat on the underside.

This piece of equipment serves four purposes:

1. When you are lowering the spinnaker to leeward it is possible to reach the spinnaker sheet—even when the spinnaker is blowing off to leeward—by pulling in the retaining line and so saving you a long journey down to the stern to retrieve the sheet.
2. When hoisting the spinnaker on a reach your retaining line can be adjusted, so that it is just short enough to stop the spinnaker sheet going over the end of the boom.
3. If you have a short-footed spinnaker up it can be used, rather like the barber hauler on the jib, for adjusting the angle of the sheet in relation to the spinnaker.
4. In very light weather on a reach or a run the line can be hooked up

on to the boom so that the block on the end of it is approximately two inches (51 mm.) from the underside. The sheet can then render easily through this and will remove any likelihood of it trailing in the water and collapsing the spinnaker.

In all cases the spinnaker sheets should run underneath the deck for two reasons, one, to reduce the windage and two, to stop the helmsman sitting on the guy when the crew is trying to adjust the tension.

Where the spinnaker sheets run through knees and over buoyancy bags, etc., one can obtain a very light nylon tube or even P.T.F.E. tube through which sheets can be run to reduce the friction on the spinnaker sheets to a minimum. If the spinnaker is on the large size, as in the Dragon, Soling or Five-point-five, where the sheet turns into the cockpit, roughly amidships, one can place a Novex block of the type which has a back plate that can be screwed down. This works well, as once again it only ratchets when there is tension, whilst when there is not it becomes a very efficient free running sheave. It is amazing the number of uses one can find for the Novex block.

The point where the spinnaker sheets come from under the sidedeck and enter the cockpit is critical as they have to be in positions where both the skipper and the crew can get at them without too much stretching. So many times have I seen the helmsman hoist the spinnaker from down aft, doing nothing while the crew sets the spinnaker boom, fastens the uphaul and downhaul, comes back into the cockpit, grabs the guy and cleats it and then pulls in the sheet! The helmsman who is 'on the ball' will, as soon as he has hoisted the spinnaker, and while the crew is fixing the spinnaker boom, adjust the guy and the sheet himself, so that it is set and pulling before his crew has finished with the boom. This saves at least ten to fifteen seconds, but is only possible if the spinnaker sheets come out at a reasonable distance from the helmsman and jamming cleats are available for him to snap these guys and sheets into immediately.

Spinnaker sheet jamming cleats

The only type of jam cleats I have found suitable for the spinnaker sheets and halyards are the small aluminium anodised jam cleats made by Holt-Allen. These, with a little attention are superb! My modification is to take them to bits and put cross grooves in them to stop the sheets and guys from working to the edge of the jam cleat when under strain (see Figure 10).

Toe straps

As I have mentioned before the main advantage in organising your own boat is that you can position items of equipment so that they fall readily to hand. Equally important it is essential to have toe straps of the right type and correctly positioned. After all, one has a difficult enough job to stay hanging out for periods of twenty minutes or so relying on brute strength alone, so we may as well make it as comfortable as possible. Probably the best way to find out the positions for everything, is to sail the boat a few times, with the crew you have teamed up with, before actually fastening on anything except the essential equipment. This will give you some idea of the positions you will be sitting in in the boat and they will vary from boat to boat and crew to crew. This is why I always advise that one should team up with a crew for at least the duration you intend taking part in top competition. If one has a heavy crew for one half of the period, then all the fittings will have to be repositioned farther aft than you had them with a light crew. To change halfway through the season to a crew of different weight could mean that he is sitting on all the fittings previously attached.

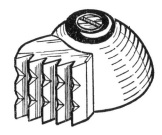

Figure 10. Cam modification to a jamming cleat to avoid accidental release.

5. Buoyancy

Types—distribution—weight—mast, boom and spinnaker boom

The subject of emergency buoyancy is a very difficult one to cover adequately as there are so many different types. In some boats buoyancy is governed by class rules, in others it is optional, but one thing is important—too much buoyancy is just as bad as too little. Why? Well, if the boat is filled with buoyancy it will float too high when on its side and if capsized to leeward, the wind pressure forces the hull towards the sail. As the sail is angled downwards the whole boat promptly turns upside down. In my opinion the correct amount of buoyancy would be sufficient so that, when the boat is capsized, the mast and centreboard are level with the water. This will enable you to climb on to the centreboard easily and it also means that the hull can drift to leeward without the boat turning upside down and, last but not least, it enables you to capsize the boat on purpose when needed. Should you have any trouble with halyards up aloft, you can simply capsize, swim up to the masthead to correct any fault, swim back to bring the boat upright and get under way again.

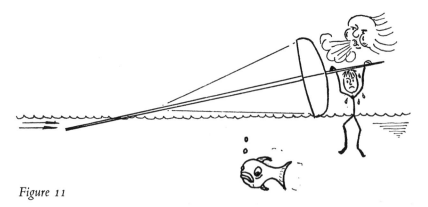

Figure 11

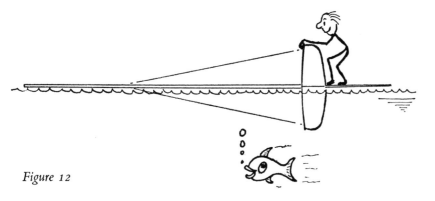

Figure 12

Transom flaps

The majority of classes now allow self bailers and transom flaps and particularly the latter are, to my mind, essential when it comes to safety. Before transom flaps were introduced, if capsized on a lee shore which could be near a cliff with a heavy sea breaking, you had to get the boat upright and bail out which would probably take five to eight minutes. Now it is possible to get upright, open the transom flaps and sail off, in possibly less than two minutes even in rough water. Because of transom flaps and self bailers the amount of buoyancy carried in boats has been reduced considerably, but I am not going to suggest the amount you carry, except that it should be sufficient to keep the gunwale of the boat when flooded, complete with all sailing gear and crew, a few inches inches above the water. If the total weight of you and your crew is very light then you can afford to have less buoyancy and vice versa if very heavy.

Whatever type of buoyancy you have it should be positioned as far away from the centreline as possible. This will have the effect of making the boat very stable when full of water. It also gives more leg room and it is usually easier to fasten bags between the hull and the deck. If you have built-in buoyancy tanks make sure all the holes are sealed since, when totally immersed, the pressure on the walls of a tank is considerable. Equally important is to have sufficient drain plugs so that if any water does get in you can find it immediately and let it out again. You could find yourself carrying water around in the buoyancy compartment without knowing it for weeks on end and wondering why you are going so slowly.

I think if I had a choice between buoyancy bags and built-in compartments I would settle for the bags. On the whole they are lighter, and if they are faulty, it can be seen immediately. They can be correctly positioned in the boat and replacements can be obtained anywhere from any one of a number of manufacturers.

Fastening buoyancy bags

The thing to remember when fastening bags into the boat is to make sure there are no sharp edges they can come in contact with, especially when the boat is full of water. The buoyancy bag pushes upwards probably against the underside of the deck and so remove any sharp bits of glue, splinters, points of screws, etc. All buoyancy bags are supplied with tags or loops, and one of the best means of fastening is to use one-and-a-half inch (38 mm.) wide nylon straps which can be screwed on to the hull with small plates and three screws to each end of the straps. These straps can then be wrapped round the bags, passed through the loops, and fastened on to the hull at each end. Whatever you do, do not fasten the bags to the boat by the tags themselves. If this happens and you capsize the force will tear the tags off and burst the bag.

Another advantage of bags is that, when laying up, the bags can be removed, thereby letting air get behind and dry out the wood which would normally stay wet if the buoyancy was built in. Some prefer to use other types of material such as polystyrene. Although this seems to be incredibly light I do not advise it since, for the amount of buoyancy you need, it is lighter to use bags. Also the polystyrene tends to soak up a fair amount of water and a good deal clings to the outside and this is one of the reasons I would suggest it is never used even inside masts.

Buoyant masts

While we are discussing buoyancy in masts I think it is interesting to point out that tests have been carried out by mast manufacturers to find out whether it is advantageous to have the mast completely sealed so that it will float, or whether it is best to have it open so that it fills with water. The tests showed that there was virtually no difference in the righting moment needed as long as there was a large enough hole at the base of a mast filled with water to drain it all out rapidly as the boat was pulled upright. Oddly enough, in this test the buoyant mast was no better at stopping the boat turning upside down than the mast that was not buoyant, therefore, I see no advantage in having a watertight mast. This is lucky because in fact it is rapidly becoming an expensive nuisance because it is very difficult to make a mast completely watertight. If you have foam in it, it adds to the weight. If you seal it off by rivets and plates it still tends to leak owing to the pressure of the water (considerable at twenty-five feet) when the mast is upside down. When brought up again the mast is half full of water without drain holes to clear it.

Another problem is the halyards in a watertight mast, they have to come down the luff rope groove or the outside of the mast. Either way is not the ideal solution and it would be much better if they could be taken straight down the centre of the mast. In this way there would be less likelihood of the halyards twisting and jamming. Many masts could be half the size of standard masts, if they did not have to be buoyant. I suppose eventually in years to come this is what will happen, but at the moment most people are obsessed about buoyant masts. It is also a general rule in France that all metal masts float.

Buoyant booms

Booms should be treated the same as masts when it comes to buoyancy and so again it does not matter whether they are buoyant or if they fill up as long as the holes at either end are capable of releasing any water immediately.

The spinnaker boom is quite different and this should float. There is always the risk of dropping it overboard and as spinnaker booms tend to be moderately expensive it is worth making sure they do float so that they may be retrieved. Spinnaker booms that leak are a menace inside the boat when they are stowed somewhere down in the bottom. When spray comes over or a few wave tops drop in, a certain amount of water is bound to lie in the bilge and if it can get into the spinnaker boom it is difficult to remove without lifting the spinnaker boom up and draining it. All this adds weight which in the end will slow you down.

6. Centreboard

Shape—finish—attachments—rake—resistance—rocking centreboard

When I first started sailing I used to think the sails were the deciding factor in whether the boat was fast or slow. Over the years this idea has receded. After discarding the sails from the top of my priority list I thought it should be the hull design, then the mast, and at present I am strongly convinced it ought to be the centreboard and rudder! This is mainly because over the past few years whenever I have had a slow boat I have changed the centreboard and the rudder, in some cases just modified the shape of them, and there has been an instant improvement in the sailing performance.

An enormous amount has already been written on this subject and the technical data which is available regarding shapes and sections would fill three books so I am going to touch very briefly on this, and give you just a little of my own experience—ideas I have put into practice and found to work.

Finish

First and foremost the board must be, as mentioned before, as smooth as it is humanly possible to make it, and I cannot emphasise this too strongly. Pay special attention to the leading and trailing edges, make sure there are no blemishes in the roundness of the leading edge. Incidentally I say 'roundness' because I feel that at no time should a leading edge be sharp, as this increases the tendency to stalling which is the major cause of lack of acceleration immediately after tacking.

Shape

Most of the outlines of the board are controlled by class rules but if there is a chance of getting rid of any sharp corners in the outline I would do so. The trailing edges of all plates need not necessarily be sharp. I have tried both a sharp and a square edge and I cannot honestly say I have noticed any difference at all except that the sharp edges do tend to break off very much easier than the blunt ones.

When making up a centreboard I would try and shape it so that it came nice and straight into a very sharp edge and, having done this and faired it all in, I would then put a plane or 'surform' straight down the edge leaving it approximately one eighth of an inch square (2 mm.). When doing this make sure the corners of the square are clean and sharp so that the water leaves the plate cleanly without any bending.

Figure 13

Rake

I feel the secret of the centreboard is in its fore and aft position in the boat. I have found that a few inches forward or a few inches aft can make an astonishing difference to the speed of the boat. When I say a few inches I do not mean the whole board, just the tip. I do not think that moving the pivot position helps at all as long as it is in approximately the right position to start with. What I do think matters is the vertical angle of the plate. I have always found that in light weather the tip of the plate should be as far forward as it will go, and as the wind gets up so it should be moved aft. This may be because, with an increase of wind there comes an increase in speed and therefore the board becomes more efficient and you need less of it. It also has the effect of reducing weather helm and because of this the boat becomes better balanced and easier to control. To my mind the centreboard should resemble the swing wing of an aircraft where one sets the wings right out on take-off but as the speed increases they are swung back in towards the body of the plane.

In the Dutchman in Force 8, we have travelled very fast to wind-ward with the plate halfway up. Admittedly, one makes a little more leeway but on the other hand it is easier to hold the boat upright because the lateral resistance is reduced and because of this the boat goes forward through the water faster. Boats which had their centreboards right down in this weight of wind were all heeling right down and making just as much leeway as we were but were not going forward fast.

One should experiment with the angle of the plate and when one has found the best position for a given strength of wind and wave condition and for the same crew weight, it should be marked for future reference. If you can experiment this way at least throughout the season you will eventually end up with a series of fixed positions for various wind strengths. It is then just a matter of putting the plate down to that mark and you will have the great advantage of knowing that you have one thing less to worry about.

Do remember that these marks are for one specific suit of sails and if you get a new suit you must start all over again. With two different suits of sails which I tried out on my Dutchman there was a difference in the best position of the centreboard in a sample wind strength of two inches. I only found this out by a fluke. Until this discovery I had blamed the sails but, of course, it was not the fault of the sails at all but merely that the centre of effort of one suit was in a different position to that of the other. Having found the new position of the plate I was then tuned to go just as fast with one suit as the other.

A few years ago Hamble River Sailing Club had a team race in G.P. Fourteens against Alderney Sailing Club, in the Channel Islands. I was allotted a boat with a radial cut sail, the only one of this cut in the fleet. As far as I remember it was a running start and I was able to get away first. We led by thirty seconds round the leeward mark, but on the following beat all the other boats stormed straight past us. I tried everything to stop this and eventually, as a last resort, I pulled up the centreboard at least a quarter of the way. Instantly the boat became alive and went much faster than the others. We won this race but I would hate to think how far behind we would have been if we had left the board right down.

I am not saying that if this is done to every G.P. that the boat will go faster. I have tried it since with a standard G.P. sail and found that it makes not the slightest difference—if anything it goes slower—but it is quite a good example of how a different cut of mainsail can alter the balance of the boat.

Centreboard position reaching

When reaching in heavy weather use less centreboard than you think you require. This point of sailing in a heavy wind resembles going to windward, where it pays if you keep your sails absolutely full and the boat upright, and the only way you can do this is by reducing the amount of lateral resistance and hence the heeling force, and I would suggest less centreboard than you normally use.

Centreboard position running

When running some crews pull the board right up inside the box. I feel this is only worth while when the wind is extremely light and speed through the water is slow. As soon as there is any wind and the speed increases, especially if there is a sea running, then the tip of the plate should always be exposed. This will help to counteract any roll and assist steering so that you can keep your boat on a straighter line using less rudder movement.

One point I have not yet covered is the occasion when going to windward in a good breeze one overstands the windward mark slightly, or it may well be that the wind has shifted and one finds one can easily make the next mark. If this is the case remember that the centreboard on these occasions, should always be slightly angled aft. Even if you are only fractionally farther off the wind than you would be if you were close hauled this small adjustment does make an enormous difference to the speed of the boat.

Attachments

There are on the market at the present time a few examples of a fitting that allows the pivot to be moved fore and aft. The only practical advantage of this fitting is that it allows you to find the correct position of the centreboard when it is set vertically in a light wind. Some crews use it in heavy weather and move the whole board aft, but I am certain that this is not right, in fact, I would go as far as to say that, having found the correct position for the pivot point of the board in light winds then I would fix it there and throw out this fitting since otherwise you might use it for adjustment unnecessarily.

Controlling the rake

How you control your centreboard is a matter of personal preference and there are many methods. I have seen it done with a bicycle chain, a handle or a large drum-type winch. All that was used on the centreboard of the Merlin Rocket class some years ago was a small friction pad and a long handle so that altering the board angle was just a matter of pushing the handle and leaving it there. Whichever method you should choose to use one thing is certain, and that is you should be able to adjust the angle of your centreboard while hanging right out. There is nothing worse than going round the windward mark with the board right down and having to stop for a few seconds while the crew gets inboard to adjust it and before setting off again. The amount of time lost during this operation is not acceptable in today's competition.

Rocking centreboard

A centreboard that is not designed to fit at an angle to the centreline, or as some people say, 'rock' should be a very tight fit in the centreboard case. The reason is to stop it twisting, which I feel is a bad thing since it could so easily twist the wrong way if you were not watching. It also stops the end of the board flapping and, most important, because of the tight fit, the water that comes into the forward end of the centreboard case cannot flow past the centreboard to the after portion. Oddly enough, because of this the water in the after portion drains out, or very nearly so. Although the amount of water removed would perhaps only weigh one and a half to two and a half pounds (1 kilo) it all makes a considerable difference.

If you want to experiment with an angling or rocking board then it must be a loose fit in the case. There are many methods of making your board angle and the most common is to have a board that is approximately three-eighths of an inch (9 mm.) smaller than the inside

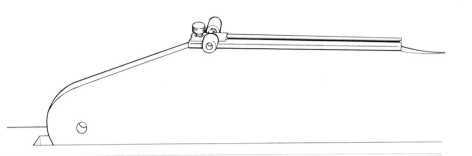

Plate 10. A simple method for ensuring that you always push the centreboard down the right amount. A small track is screwed to the back edge of the centreboard where it enters the centreboard case. The slide has a locking plunger and the 'tee' piece rests against the top of the centreboard case thus preventing it being lowered too far.

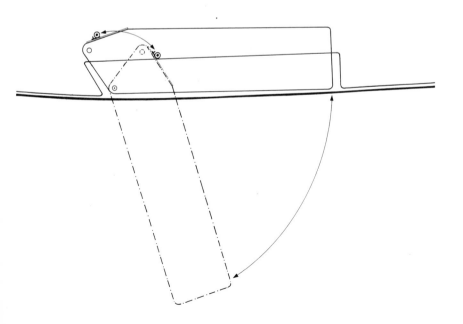

Plate 11. When reaching under spinnaker in light weather it pays for the helmsman to sit to leeward with the crew right out on the wire but I do not think the increase in speed is due solely to the fact that the crew can see the spinnaker better. Note how the spinnaker guy is led on this boat. It has been hooked under the weather gunwale just by the shrouds and this keeps it well clear of the trapeze artist and allows him to move in and out freely.

width of the case. Pack the after edge of the board with tufnol strip or similar material so that the after edge is then held in the centre of the gap in the case, whilst the forward edge is free to move from side to side. Now, when sailing to windward, the pressure on the leeward side of the board forces the forward edge up to the weather side of the case, thus angling your board to windward of the centreline of the boat. This does not have the effect of driving you up to windward as so many people think. All it does is to reduce the amount of leeway made. Against this there is a little more resistance and you will have to drive the boat a lot harder to make up for it and, in certain conditions, such as in a choppy sea when you cannot get maximum speed out of your boat, it certainly does not pay to angle the centreboard.

If you use an angling board remember when the board is half raised that the tufnol strips that hold it centrally in the case will be exposed above the top of the case and the board will be able to flap around uncontrolled. On a reach this has the disastrous effect of making the boat roll. One way of avoiding this is to place two vertical strips of tufnol on the inside of the case just aft of the point where the board would be in the normal position when going to windward. As you pull the board up it will enter the slot between the two pads and will still be held tightly.

Resistance

To enable the board to be pulled up and down easily it is worth while lining the inside of the case with P.T.F.E. as well as the edges of the board itself and also the part inside the case. This should only be done in the area where the board touches when the boat is going to windward as there is no point in carrying the P.T.F.E. too far aft. This would just mean excess weight and does not help the movement of the board at all.

7. Rudder

Faults—pintles—tiller length, extension and joint—shape—finish—rake—resistance—lifting and fixed

I have always considered the rudder to be rather like the front wheel of a bicycle for the following reasons:

1. They are both a means of turning the vehicle.
2. They are both used to adjust the balance of the vehicle when going very fast.
3. If very high speeds are reached a 'speed wobble' will be set up.
4. Any resistance in the rudder or wheel will slow you down.
5. If a rudder is not large enough, it is like having treadless tyres, and eventually you will fall over.
6. The connection between the blade and the tiller extension must be positive. Imagine trying to ride a bicycle with the handlebars only loosely connected to the wheel.
7. If used to excess both will act as a brake.

To elaborate on the above points:

The rudder allows you to steer the boat on any given course; simply by pushing or pulling the tiller to move the angle of the rudder blade in the water, and because of the water pressure set up on one side or the other, the rudder blade then moves the stern. When racing in close quarters you make great demands on the rudder to guide you accurately through small gaps, and to get out of other people's way, possibly when they may be out of control! I have often felt that too many people take the rudder for granted, and just hang it on the stern without worrying too much about how it is attached, or its shape, etc.

Faults

The majority of boats looked at in the dinghy park have rudder pintles that are either out of line or are slack, so that when the rudder is placed on them they are either not vertical, or they rattle around loosely. You will also find rudders with the bottoms of the leading edge furred up where they have run aground and the owner has not worried about cleaning them up again; rudders that are badly warped because they are painted with a dark colour, and so on.

Make sure there is no play at all in the rudder cheeks, if you have a lifting rudder. The best way to get rid of this is by putting a wing nut on the end of the pivot bolt, and then you can screw it up to clamp the cheeks to the blade when the rudder is in the down position.

Resistance

I have seen many rudders that are hung too low, so that the cheeks are in the water. When you are sailing it is very difficult to see properly, but next time you are planing fast have a look at the stern, and if there are a couple of water spouts up either side of the rudder it is an absolute certainty that your rudder is slung too low. The easiest way to get over this problem is not by altering the shape of the rudder cheeks, but by moving the pintles further up the transom. This may mean you have to cut a bit off the head of the rudder, but so what—more weight lost.

Balance

It would be impossible to ride a bicycle, even in a straight line, with a fixed front wheel. In just the same way, when going reasonably fast in a dinghy, you rely on constant small movements of the rudder to keep the boat balanced upright. When I say this I am assuming that everything else in the boat is tuned to perfection: the centreboard in the right place, main boom at the right angle and the crew in the right position. This balancing effect is achieved because, when the angle of the rudder is moved from the centreline, the water pressure on the side of the rudder is creating a lever, and the best way to see how this works is for you to try moving the tiller backwards and forwards slowly the next time you are sailing on a run in medium weather. This will make the boat roll since, if you push the tiller away from you, the force of the water on the side of the rudder will try to make the rudder blade go the same way as the tiller, and this tends to make the boat tip to windward.When you are going very fast this becomes very much more effective, which brings me to the next point.

Rake

When you are sailing at extreme planing speeds, and it becomes more a matter of survival, there is a likelihood that the boat will set up what I call a 'speed wobble', identical to what happens to a bicycle going downhill too fast. I have tried to find out why this occurs, and after experimenting I believe that the vertical angle of the rudder plays a big part in it. With a rudder that is very nearly vertical one normally has great control over the direction of the boat, without much force being applied to the tiller. I think it is because of this that the speed wobble comes about and it is caused by the rudder blade flapping slightly. This can be immediately corrected by angling the blade slightly further aft. It will of course make it much harder to steer, but the rudder will follow the water flow better, since the centre of effort has now been moved further aft in relation to the pivot point, i.e. the pintles. When I say move the blade aft I am only suggesting that you move the tip of the blade an inch or two inches (25 or 51 mm.), and not more.

Finish

Because of the pressure that is exerted on the side of the blade it is essential that the surface finish on the rudder is perfect.

Shape

The trailing edge can be a little thinner than the trailing edge of the centreboard, but again it should be squared off if possible. The leading edge, however, has to be quite different from that of the centreboard, since it often works at a greater angle of attack to the water flow. This means that the leading edge of the rudder has to be rounder, especially at the top of the blade where it ought to be positively fat and then thin out gradually towards the bottom of the blade. Near the tip it should be blunt but thin and rather bullet-shaped.

Many people think that the leading edge of the rudder should be sharp. I have always found that this induces stalling. I mean by this that when the rudder is turned the water does not flow round this sharp leading edge, so that turbulence is created on the low-pressure side which breaks down the smooth flow over the rest of the blade, and the rudder loses a great deal of its effect. If the leading edge is nice and blunt but rounded, the water flow can follow the surface without breaking away and therefore the stalling will not occur. There are two other ways in which a rudder can stall; first, if you slam the tiller over very hard it does not give the water time to flow evenly over the blade and this will cause it to stall. This is very noticeable in some keel boats with separate spade rudders. A good example is the Soling. Just try bearing away violently in a Soling and all that happens is that the tiller goes very light, and you hear a big gurgling under the stern, while the boat just goes straight on but a little slower than before. The second case occurs when the rudder blade is not big enough, and this brings us to the next point.

Size

You know how difficult it is to ride a bicycle with a worn-down, old treadless tyre, especially in wet weather—it is downright danger-ous. Try turning a corner and the front wheel will go straight on; and it is just the same with a too small rudder. If your rudder blade is not big enough you will have no control over the boat when it is blowing hard. You will find that you are planing along merrily, flat out, the bows will hit a wave, she will start luffing up, you will pull the tiller up to correct it and . . . nothing happens . . . just a big hole in the water and the boat will continue coming up into the wind . . . and . . . splash, you will be swimming!

For many years it has been said that the 'river boys', i.e. the crews sailing on the inland waters and rivers, do not stand a chance when it comes to sailing in a blow at sea. I have often felt this is caused by the fact that when on the river you very seldom need a big rudder. Nine times out of ten the weather is light and there are seldom any waves, therefore the size of the rudder they use is adequate, and also reduces wetted surface and weight. Unfortunately, they try to use the same rudder when they go to a regatta or championship held in open waters. I am afraid this just does not work, and so I think it much better to have two rudders, one for inland waterways or for light air at sea and a second rudder, very much larger, for use when it blows.

The Dutchman class in North America have rather a good idea, where the rudder cheeks are rather like a daggerboard case, and the daggerboard is the rudder itself. When the wind is light they put the daggerboard down halfway, and when it blows they put it right down. In this way they can get just the amount of area they require at any time with only one rudder.

Pintles and joints

Back to the bicycle again. How about riding a bicycle with handlebars so loose that they would not move the front wheel until they are turned two or three inches? I do not suppose you would last very long. Well, it is the same as having a tiller, and tiller extension, that has play in the joints. There are four points to attend to. The first we have already covered, which is the cheeks of the rudder if it is of a lifting type.

The second place where play can be introduced is in the pintles. Slop here causes the rudder to flop sideways and induces rolling when sailing downwind.

Thirdly, where the tiller enters the rudder head it must be fixed absolutely rigidly and I cannot emphasise too strongly that there should be no movement here whatsoever. It does not matter whether you screw it, glue it, clamp it, or even have the tiller a part of the rudder hood, but it must not move at all. It goes without saying that the fourth joint, the tiller extension connection or swivel, should be slop-free as well. I am afraid I cannot give photos of good types, because all those I have seen on the market at present have play in one direction or another. It may be that by the time this book is printed someone will realise the importance of this and produce a good one.

The tiller extension joints I have used have all been made from parts of goosenecks which, oddly enough, work very well, although they are a little heavy. This is, I think, a case of where one has to make one's own coupling. Tiller extensions themselves are quite important, in that they have to be long enough to push the tiller right down to leeward without the helmsman coming in off the weather rail. Usually tiller extensions are only just long enough to reach the weather rail, and if you want to push down to leeward you have to lean in. I suggest a good all round length for a tiller extension is one that projects fourteen inches (35 cm.) beyond the edge of the boat.

If you have a little 'T' piece on the end of the tiller, throw it away. The number of capsizes I have seen caused by this catching in oilskin pockets are too numerous to mention. It is much better to have a 'V'-shaped piece of ply glued on to the end, or better still, ping-pong balls. In fact, you can use anything that will not catch in the side of the boat or your clothing.

Braking and propelling

Because of the pressure which builds up on the side of the rudder when you want the boat to turn, the rudder will be acting as a brake also, and it is important, therefore, to use the rudder as little as possible. This, of course, is not so in light weather, when you can waggle the tiller vigorously and push the boat extremely fast to windward or in any direction!

Figure 14. A tiller extension joint made from a gooseneck.

During my first international regatta in San Remo I was laying the windward mark nicely with another boat to leeward, who could not possibly make the mark. 'Aha,' I thought, 'I've got him.' My joy was short lived because, as we approached the mark and he found he could not lay it, he started waggling the tiller madly when head to wind . . . and shot round the mark a good twenty feet ahead of me! Somewhat disillusioned, I realised that the only way to win races abroad without cheating was to have a very much faster boat. You will probably say, why did I not protest? But how can you prove a chap is waggling his tiller? It is only your word against his and the likely outcome of this protest would be dismissal on lack of evidence.

Although this is a good example of what can happen in light weather, in heavy weather one cannot waggle the rudder fast enough to get any forward movement, as the rudder is being pulled through the water faster than it can propel itself. Therefore, tiller waggling is reversed, and it then creates a resistance. I have found in the past that, on dead runs before the wind when one very seldom has to move the tiller to keep the boat on the straight and narrow path, if one sits on the tiller extension with the tiller amidships, there is no play in the rudder at all. The speed of the boat is therefore increased considerably.

One last word on rudders, do not forget to lock the rudder on. If you capize and it falls off, that is that and there is no way of continuing the race, and it can also be dangerous.

8. Underwater Attachments

Keel bands—slot-rubbers—bilge keels

Underwater attachments and fittings are, luckily, few in number and at present most of the thought put into boats seems to be for attention to the inside of the hull, rather than the underside. But the underwater fittings are more important.

Keel bands

Let us start with the keel bands. I would suggest that they are left off altogether on dinghies, if the class rules will allow this. The keel band is a left-over from the good old days, when they had half-inch brass strip round the underside so that you could pull the boat up the hard or the shingle without damage. Nowadays, with modern trailers and the care people take with their boats, I think keel bands are a waste of time. On the other hand, we have to consider them because there are still some outdated class rules which say they have to be fitted to the boat.

If this is the case in your class, then first of all make sure that they are the smallest allowed by the rules, and that they are also made up from the lightest permissible material. In the majority of cases this would be either aluminium, tufnol or other reinforced resin. These materials are expensive and sometimes difficult to get hold of but are well worth the extra trouble.

The shape of the keel band has often worried me. I am not quite sure which shape is the best, if it should be a half-round or whether it should be a rectangle, and probably it does not matter. One thing is certain and that is that, when fitting the keel band, it must be exactly in the centre of the boat and dead straight. The easiest way to fit it is first to pin a piece of cotton to the base of the stem on the centre-line and stretch it to a post which has been clamped to the centreline of the transom. Arrange it so that it is just clear of the keel and it is then easy to fasten the keel band to the boat, exactly under the piece of cotton. Epoxy resin glue and brass pins are the best materials for fastening, but you should only glue it down in areas where the keel band will not need to be removed at any time, and these are usually the parts fore and aft of the centreboard case. Where the keel band goes alongside the centreboard slot and over the top of the slot-rubbers, screws should be used. If you then have any difficulties later with torn slot-rubbers it will be easy enough to replace them.

Slot-rubbers

While on the subject of slot-rubbers, it is essential to use a thick, soft type of material. I suggest at least three-sixteenths inches (4 mm.) thick neoprene, which is unaffected by sea water. If it is possible to slot out the bottom inside edge of the centreboard case neoprene slot-rubbers will not only keep out the water very effectively, but will last for at least two to three years, given proper treatment. (see Figure 15). When fastening the slot-rubbers to the boat, rub down the part they are to lie on, cleaning with a cleaning fluid, and stick the rubber on with rubber-based adhesive. When this is dry and hardened it is then possible to put the keel bands in position and screw them down on the rubber without it moving.

The slot-rubber can be made up of two pieces fixed independently either side of the slot, or of just one piece. The latter, when it is

Figure 15. A section of a centreboard case showing how the slot rubbers should be arranged.

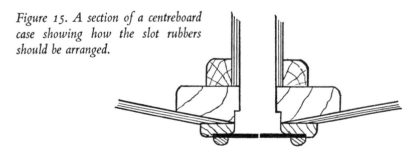

glued down and fastened with the keel band can then be slit with a razor blade. I know that it is generally thought necessary to have overlapping slot rubbers to keep out the water, but if you have a thick enough, soft enough, piece of neoprene you only need the two halves just to touch. The other advantage of slitting with a razor blade is that you need only slit it where the centreboard operates, leaving the parts fore and aft of this position in one piece. If you do it this way, find the position of the centreboard when right down and drill a hole in the slot-rubber level with the edge of the board, and repeat at the after end. Slit the rubber in between the two holes and this way it will be unlikely to tear at the end of the slits.

There are many boats being fitted with double slot-rubbers, i.e. two layers of thin rubber under the keel band, and some even have a length of sponge placed on the inside of the box at the bottom, but I think these methods are not as good as the plain thick neoprene. Beware of the rubber that has any form of cloth moulded in it as this will shrink and cause the rubber to crinkle.

If you must grease the slot-rubbers to keep them supple the only thing I have found to be any good is castor oil! Any other form of lubrication usually destroys the rubber.

At each end of the centreboard slot there should be a plate which is triangular in shape and fairs in the single keelband at each end of the boat with the double keel band at the slot, and also holds down the forward end of the slot-rubbers. It is important that this is correctly bedded in and shaped so that it parts the water with the minimum of effort.

All screw heads should be facing the same way, i.e. slots fore-and-aft, and these slots should be filled up with epoxy resin and rubbed over with fine wet-and-dry paper.

Bilge keels

Bilge keels, if you must have them under class rules, should be as small as possible and made from the lightest materials. It is important to pay attention to the fore-and-aft ends of the bilge keels to make sure that everything is done to divert the water flow slowly and smoothly. There should be no corners or sharp radii.

An interesting fitting thought up by Peter Milne who, I believe, fitted it into the prototype Fireball, was a small piece of stainless strip which fitted into the after end of the centreboard case with approximately a quarter of an inch (6 mm.) projecting below the slot-rubber. The idea of this was that it would act as a self bailer and when the boat was moving forward it would lower the level in the aft end of the centreboard case. I understand that this worked very well but for some unknown reason does not seem to have been used since.

9. Masts

Requirements—weight—windage—centre of gravity—fittings—spreaders— accessories

When stating your preference for a new mast it is worth remembering that the basic requirement is that it should perform as intended. This really means that it should be flexible enough for you to hold the boat upright in a blow with a light all-up crew weight, or to be stiff enough to stop the sail going out of shape if the all-up crew weight is on the heavy side. Some masts have to bend to leeward at the top and to windward at the middle, especially those which carry rigs with large overlapping foresails. This is not necessarily advantageous in classes where the jib has no overlap, and again your requirements will be entirely different for a boat that has no jib.

Types of masts available

Having decided on how you feel the mast should perform to the crew weight available, there are three ways of obtaining this mast. First of all remember the three 'Golden Rules' in order of importance,

Plate 12. This crew appears to be unaware that anything nasty is happening above him! Surprisingly, this Tempest survived the gusts. But what has happened? In most cases if the mast top goes over the bow, the middle usually comes aft, but in this case the middle has gone forward as well. Is it the shrouds which are stretched or is it that the boat itself is flexing?

Plate 13. Although it is blowing hard the Soling mast on the left of the picture should not bend in this way. The lower shrouds are too tight and are holding the middle of the mast up to windward. This type of bend can be induced by over-tightening the backstay. If you must have a tight backstay you must loosen the lower shrouds even more.

i.e. minimum weight, minimum windage and minimum (lowest) centre of gravity (C.G.).

The first way of solving your mast problem would be to have one of large diameter, but with very thin walls which will make it extremely light.

The second extreme would be to have it made with a very small diameter; but to get it as stiff as mast number one you would have to have very thick walls, which means it would be much heavier.

The third alternative would be a very small diameter with very thin walls, therefore making it a light section but, to achieve the stiffness required, it would have to be fitted with diamond bracing or jumper struts and this would increase the windage.

The performance of the three masts would be very similar. They would more or less have the same stiffness, and if they have been properly designed, which we will assume is the case, the difference between the three can be broken down into weight, windage and C.G. position.

In the first mast you have an extremely light spar, but rather large in diameter. This large diameter will of course create a certain amount of turbulence. The second type of mast is very small in diameter, reducing the turbulence but, on the other hand, is very much heavier, which will increase the all-up weight of the boat. The third is very small in diameter and very light but, to achieve the same stiffness, has a mass of spreaders, diamonds, etc., which will not only increase the windage but will create turbulence.

I find it very difficult to lay down any hard and fast rule as to which of these masts is the best. My own feeling is that, in order to have a mast of minimum weight, I would suffer the extra size of the section. Many of my friends feel that the weight in a mast does not make too much difference in a dinghy, as it is supposed to be kept upright. One has to remember though, that it is very seldom that one gets round the course without the dinghy pitching to some extent and the movement of a heavy mast high up is enough to upset the balance of any boat.

In the case of keel boats it has been proved time and time again that it is necessary to have the lightest mast that will stand up, although there are one or two leading designers in the world who still specify masts considerably stronger than really needed.

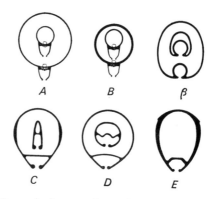

A and B are both manufactured by Needlespar.
C is an Elvstrom Section.
D is Proctor 'B' and Beta is Proctor Beta.
E an Australian Section marketed by Craig Whitworth.

The one thing Sections A, B, C and D have in common, is that they all have approximately the same moments of inertia, in other words, if you were to support them between two trestles, and hang 'X' number of pounds on each one, you would find the amount of deflection would be approximately the same.

But we are still left with the question, which section is the best. Figure B has without doubt, the minimum windage, but on the other hand it is excessively heavy. Figure C is a little lighter but it is larger than the previous section. Figures A and D, offer the lightest possible section but because of the increased size, there will be more windage. What is intriguing, is that by altering the shape of a section, as in Beta, the stiffness or moment of inertia can be considerably increased. Although the section itself is not excessively heavy and it is smaller than all but Figure B.

Figure E is the latest Section to come out of Australia and is designed by Bob Miller and Craig Whitworth. It is a very small section which has average moment of inertia, and is very heavy. In many ways it resembles Figure B. One interesting feature is the lip on either side of the forward edge. I understand that this is put there to encourage turbulent flow on the leeward side of the mast which, in theory, reduces the amount of drag.

All these sections can be used with the minimum amount of

Plates 14, 15 and 16. Three types of mast bend control. Top left is John Truett's device which has the merit of being lockable and accurately calibrated. The rack and pinion, top right, is instantly adjustable, but the control line can stretch. At the bottom is Cliff Norbury's device which can be calibrated, but again the line can stretch.

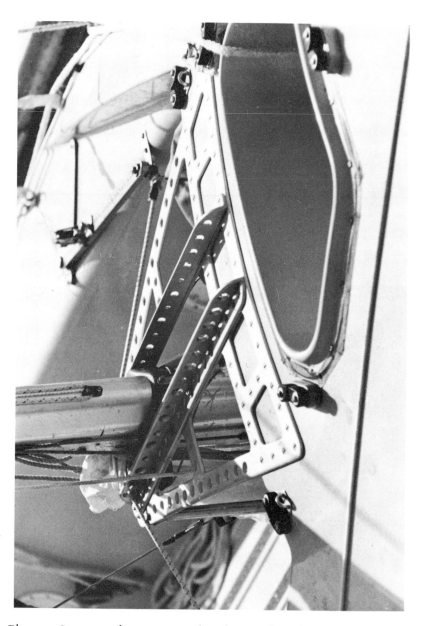

Plate 17. Some people go to great lengths to reduce the all-up weights of their boats but even so this mast gate on a Tempest is a work of art which is an example to us all that no part of the boat should be neglected in this respect.

rigging, i.e. limited swing spreaders, as described in the rigging section.

The smaller section, inside these drawings, is the section at the top of the mast. You will see that the only one with any notable difference is Figure C, but I still think that lateral stiffness at this point is an asset because it means you can tighten your boom vang and therefore have a tight leach on your mainsail when reaching. However, time will tell whether this view is right or not.

Windage

The one certain thing is that the thin mast which is light, but has to have plenty of rigging to make it stand up, is definitely wrong. The windage of this mast is considerable. A good example of this is the old Fourteen Foot International mast that had two sets of diamonds and jumpers as well. It was an effort to hold this mast upright when putting it into the boat in a breeze. It is not only the windage we are concerned about; it is what happens to the air flow once it has passed the rigging, where all those little turbulent eddies go streaming back astern like cobwebs. The effect this has on the mainsail drive is disastrous.

As I have settled for the mast of minimum weight it is now essential to try and reduce the windage. This can be done by removing all the external halyards and cordage and, in keel boats, remove also cleats, winches, etc. In fact, remove everything possible above deck level. If it is not possible to remove any of these items it may be well worth putting a guard of aerofoil section, made from something like fibreglass, round them. This will reduce the windage and also the turbulence over the rest of the hull.

Masthead

The masthead should be light with no sharp projections. If it is possible to get the burgee halyard inside, then do so. The burgee in most cases is far too large, it should be cut down to the minimum size required by the rules. Many keel boats have a wind indicator and wind speed fitting stuck on an arm. This is usually made of round tube which has a high wind resistance and could well be made from a streamlined strut. No doubt the strut would be larger than the tube, but as long as it had an aerofoil section the resistance would be less. All shrouds and forestay attachments should be internal and the same fitting method should be used for the lower shrouds as well, if they are fitted.

Spreaders

Spreaders should be of the aerofoil type and the section should be angled downwards. The amount of downward tilt depends on the average amount the boat heels, i.e. if the heel on your boat averages ten degrees then the angle of the spreaders should be down by ten degrees. This enables the wind to flow directly over the spreaders, causing the minimum of turbulence.

Figure 16. A simple method of fitting the top end of shrouds internally. The belled-over stainless steel tube has less windage than a nut on a threaded bolt.

Figure 17. Showing the arrangement of aerofoil section spreaders to give the smallest possible overall wind resistance.

Turbulence

While on the subject of turbulence, I feel that even more important than windage is the cutting down on the amount of turbulence you are creating over the mainsail. We have done this to a certain extent by getting rid of the halyards and putting the shroud attachments inside. We can also reduce it by tapering the mast at the top, where the section should be as small as possible. Not only does this cut down the weight and lower the C.G. but, because it is so much smaller, the turbulence is less and this is very important at this point, because the cross-measurement of the mainsail here is also small, and it is vital that turbulence should not extend too far and make this part of the mainsail quite ineffective. The small top will also make the mast bend a little more, but not as much as some people would think, because the pull of the mainsail at this point is very nearly directly downwards. The amount of mast above the top black band should also be kept down to the absolute minimum. The majority of sheave cages at the top of masts are much too big and could be halved on most masts.

Main halyard hook-up

I have never thought there was much to be gained by having a main halyard hook-up. I know that I am in the minority in this view, but I have always felt that masts without hook-ups, probably owing to extra compression load, bend far more evenly through their length than the ones with the hook-up.

Fitting a mast to a sail

It still astonishes me to hear of people taking their boat to the sailmaker and rigging it for him, so that the sailmaker can make a sail to suit the mast. This is a ridiculous situation, for how can the sail-maker be expected to do this with a boat sitting outside his loft with virtually no side strain on the rig and just the tension of the mainsheet bending the mast. There is no weight on the shrouds, no righting moment, no flexing of the mast when the boat hits a wave, no back-winding caused by the jib . . . and yet they think this is the best way to go about having a new sail made. It is not!

Most sailmakers in England now are experts at turning out a sail that will go fast. What you have to do is accept this sail, put it in your boat and tune the mast to fit the sail. This can be done by various means which are quite difficult to explain, but nevertheless I will try.

Mast bend

As mentioned before, it is essential that you should tune the mast whilst always using the same crew weight. This is most important, as it will tell you the exact amount of mast bend you require.

If you are one of those unlucky people with a different crew each week-end, then I would say it is almost impossible to tune the mast accurately. The amount of bend you will require will also alter according to the wind strength. You really need it to bend enough to flatten the mainsail to a hard-wind shape, to open up the slot so that you can hold the boat up with the crew weight available in a reasonable amount of wind. But, should the wind drop, you want the mast to stiffen automatically so that it closes the slot, tightens the leach of the mainsail and makes it fuller, thereby giving you much more driving force. In fact, if everything is right, you will find that you will then be hanging out just as hard as you would be in heavy winds.

In very light airs one has to induce the mast to bend, or release the bend control device so that it may take up the natural bend. How much bend there is will be dictated by the mainsail you are using and it is up to you to experiment to find out the amount of bend needed to make you go fast.

I would point out, before starting on how to control the bend in your mast, regardless of what you may have heard about a mast bending fore-and-aft and athwartships, it does not happen quite like this in practice. If you can visualise yourself being directly above a boat when it is going to windward you would find that the mast bends neither sideways nor fore-and-aft, but at an angle to the centre line. This bend is caused by the middle of the mast flexing forward and the top going back and to leeward. Because the middle of the mast is flexing forward this slackens off the shrouds and the forestay slightly and the slackened rigging, together with the thrust from the gooseneck, tends to make the mast bend at an angle to the centreline.

The best bend for your type of boat, sails and crew weight, is, of course, impossible to say. This can only be found by trial and error, but it is possible on the modern mast to be able to get any combination that you may require.

To run through the factors that govern this I will start at deck level:

Mast gate

Assuming that the mast is keel stepped, how it is held at deck level plays an important part in how the mast will bend in the lower half.

First, the mast must not be able to move sideways in the mast gate
(the partners). It should be a sliding fit, and the mast gate itself should
be rigidly fixed to the boat. Make sure the sides that are touching the
mast are lined with some very hard material, such as tufnol or cloth-
reinforced phenolic resin, that cannot wear appreciably as the season
goes on. On the forward side of the mast there should be a certain
amount of clearance. This will allow the mast to flex, especially when
thumping into a head sea. Just how much clearance should be allowed
is difficult to say, but if you fix it so that it cannot move at all at this
point you will have virtually a straight mast.

Gooseneck

Moving a little way up the mast we come to the gooseneck. This
plays quite an important part in the bending of the mast, especially
in those classes that allow different heights for the mainsails, i.e.
Snipe, Flying Dutchman, etc. In the Dutchman class, for example,
there can be a difference of very nearly twelve inches (305 mm.)
between the uppermost position and the lower. It is strange that when
it is blowing very hard most people lower their mainsails to the
bottom black band to reduce the heeling moment, which in itself
is correct, but this has the effect of lowering the gooseneck position,
which is then nearer the mast gate and the mast becomes considerably
stiffer. If the mast is stiffer, so the mainsail is fuller and you are back at
'square one'!

Forget about dropping down to the lower black band in hard winds
—it is far better to stick to one position even if it is the top one. The
gooseneck causes the mast to bend by the thrust of the boom, and
this thrust is created by the kicking strap, the mainsheet and the sail.
You have probably seen what happens to your mast when tightening
the kicking strap winch, although some of this is the top of the mast
coming back, the majority is the boom thrusting the middle of the
mast forward. The same thing happens when you haul in on the
mainsheet.

Main sheet angle

Let us for example think of the centre mainsheet. If, when going
to windward with a centre mainsheet, one can normally pull the

boom down far enough to take the strain off the kicking strap, then the thrust via the gooseneck partly relies on the angle that the mainsheet comes off the boom. If you were to slide the attachment points of the mainsheet aft along the boom you would make the mast bend very much more than if you had them straight above the traveller. The exact opposite would occur if you moved the attachment points further forward. I have found with the new light-sectioned masts, that it is worth moving the attachment points aft in light weather to induce the mast to bend. When it blows hard and there is enough wind to bend the mast on its own, it is worth sliding the mainsheet attachment points further forward, taking some of the gooseneck load off the mast.

Cunningham hole

Whilst thinking about this area of the spar we have the cunningham hole. If you have a very light and flexible mast make sure that you have a very stretchy luff mainsail, or else when you tighten up the cunningham hole in a blow enormous compression loads are put on the mast.

Fully swinging spreaders

Continuing our survey of control points we come to the spreaders. First we will look at the fully swinging type, i.e. the ones that are just hinged to the mast and can swing from directly forward of the mast, round one side, to directly aft (see Figure 18). This type of spreader should always work in tension. If at any time it should come

Figure 18. A method of fixing spreaders to a mast so that they are free swinging. They should be set up so that they are always in tension.

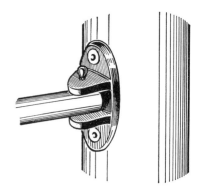

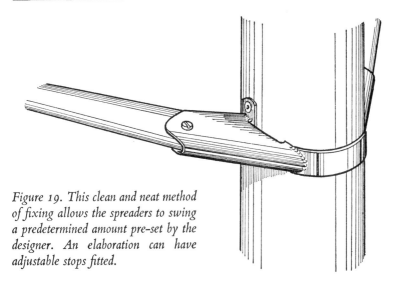

Figure 19. This clean and neat method of fixing allows the spreaders to swing a predetermined amount pre-set by the designer. An elaboration can have adjustable stops fitted.

under compression there is a possibility, because there is no restriction on the swinging movement of the spreader, that the middle of the mast can pop back. This sometimes happens when running in a heavy wind with the spinnaker up. Swinging spreaders rely a great deal on the tension of the shroud to give the mast the support that is needed. Basically, what it amounts to is that the longer the spreader, the more the mast will bend and the shorter the spreader the stiffer the mast.

Limited swing spreaders

I am pleased to say that the swinging spreader is going out of fashion, and in its place is coming what is known as the limited swing spreader which gives far more control over the bending characteristics of the mast (see Figure 19).

This works in two ways: (1) the length of the spreader arm and, (2) the angle that this arm is swept aft. Usually this angle can be regulated by the small pins at the inboard end of the bracket. I personally would recommend that all dinghies or keel boats using this type of spreader bracket, having once found the correct angle, should lock this spreader so that it can neither swing forwards nor backwards. This helps when running in a hard wind, when the centre of the mast may well try and blow backwards under the pull of the spinnaker higher up.

Controlling mast bend by spreaders

On dinghies, a point to remember about the limited swing spreader is that if you want the mast to be stiff, then the spreaders should push the shroud out of line by at least two and a half inches (6 cm.). They then have to be angled forward so that the outboard end pulls the shroud forward out of line by up to one and a quarter inches (3 cm.) which has the effect of holding the mast rigidly. Now, should you require the mast to bend, but only to bend at an angle close to the fore and aft line, then the spreader length should remain the same, but the angle on the spreader should be brought aft (see Figure 20). This allows the centre of the mast to go forward, but because the spreader is so long there is considerable side thrust which persuades the mast to keep near to the centreline.

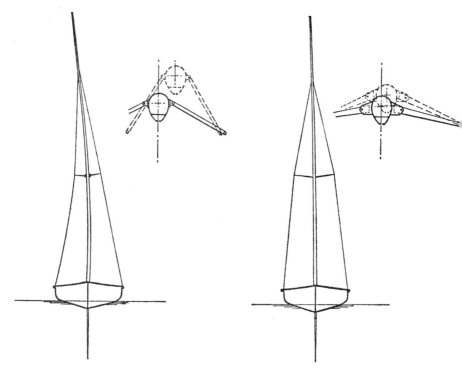

Figure 20. Using free swinging spreaders, the mast on the left moves forward and to windward in the middle a large amount. On the right the mast moves until the spreaders come up against the stops and the rig is thus stiffened at this point.

Plate 18. By moving the point where the shroud meets the deck it is possible to alter the bending characteristics of the mast. Moving the shroud inboard stiffens the mast athwartships and vice versa. The problem is how to do it when you are afloat. Here, a small tufnol insert has a number of notches in it. To move the shroud the tufnol insert is lifted out and the shroud is slipped into another notch.

Plate 19, below. John Truett's method which has a spring-loaded plunger.

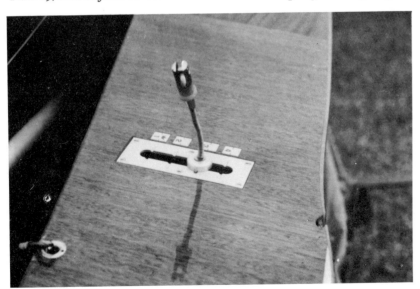

Plates 20 and 21. John Truett's magnificent Flying Dutchman machinery for adjusting the position of the heel of the mast, for tightening or slacking the genoa halyard, tensioning the boom vang, and much more besides!

Now, if you want the mast to bend at a greater angle to the centreline so that the slot can be opened up, then the spreader will have to be shortened and the angle left the same. The middle of the mast will then take up a greater angle to the centreline and looking from aft will give the impression it is bowing directly up to windward.

Jib leach affecting mast bend

When testing this while sailing it is worth remembering that the leach of your jib plays an important part in bending the mast. If your jib has a very tight or hooked leach this will induce the mast to have a greater angle of bend, whereas a very slack leach will have the opposite effect. The reason for this is that when the mainsail is full of wind and the luff is not lifting at all, the tensions in the cloth along the luff length are trying to hold the mast back. This, therefore, will stop it bending excessively, but as soon as you sheet in the jib which has a tight leach, and is creating a very small slot, the mainsail starts backwinding which instantly reduces the cloth tension and allows the mast to bend.

Shroud tension

Shroud tension plays an important part in mast bend, but not quite as much as the swinging spreader. You will find that with both types of spreader, tightening your shrouds allows the mast to bend less and this is because you are giving more support to the spreaders. This leads us to the importance of shroud levers.

In a race, if you want your mast to bend differently it is, of course, impracticable to climb up the mast and alter the length and angle of the spreaders. You have a choice of altering the vertical angle of the mainsheet, by altering the position of the blocks on the boom or, more effective, adjusting the tension of your shrouds. If you ease the shroud the mast will bend more. This is especially marked in light weather when on a long leg it is worth while tightening the leeward shroud lever and letting go of the windward one. This will let the mast fall over to leeward which, for some unknown reason, makes the boat go faster. I was once watching some sand yachts and I found that they too let the mast lean over to leeward so there must be something in it.

Mainsail and mast bend

Mainsails play quite an important part in the bending of the mast. When one is trying to tune a rig one should stick to one mainsail and not chop and change because, for example, a fuller mainsail allows the mast to bend more than a flat one. I have often heard complaints at the end of the season that aluminium masts are getting soft. The owner states that they have not touched anything since they first started sailing. They are using the same sails, same crew weight, same tension on the shrouds but the mast is bending much more. And they are right! So often you put a new boat in the water, tune it up and it goes very fast, only to lose its edge as the season proceeds. It is only recently that the cause of this has been found. It is nothing to do with the mast going soft or anything like that. It is caused by the tenon in the bottom of the mast.

Mast step

When the boat is new this tenon is a tight fit into the heel plug or adjustable mast step or whatever fitting is being used but, because of the force that is applied to the end of the limited swing spreaders by the shroud, the mast is continually trying to twist, first to one side then to the other, according to which tack you are on. This gradually and eventually wears either the tenon or the mortice in which the tenon sits. As soon as this happens, it allows the mast to twist and because the mast is twisting, the end of the spreader moves aft which reduces the effectiveness of the spreader itself and hence the mast bends differently.

The way to avoid this is to use an adjustable mast step made from a short length of channel with holes in it. By putting a bolt through the channel at either end of the tenon and clamping them up hard it is impossible for the mast heel to move. All this came to light because it was found that the people who were complaining that their masts were not as good as when new were the ones with limited swing spreaders. It is very seldom that this problem occurs with masts without this type of spreader.

Figure 21

Angle of boom to centreline

One point worth noting here is that when running in a heavy wind the mast relies on the gooseneck to push this part forward so that it will counteract the forward pull at the top. Now, if you let your boom right out against the shroud, not only do you lever the mast aft because of the pivoting action where the boom touches the shroud, but the thrust on the gooseneck is nearly at right angles to the

*Figure 22. If the boom is allowed to
rest on the shroud when running, the
force transmitted to the gooseneck tries
to lever the middle of the mast aft, with
a danger of breakage.*

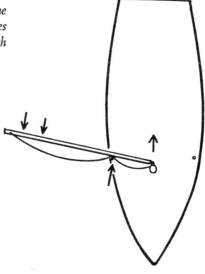

centreline, so that there is little to stop the mast reversing itself, i.e.
the centre will come aft. The only way to stop this is to make a
'Golden Rule' that you never let the boom out to the shrouds in
anything but light airs. In any case, I do not think it is necessary to let
it out very far when it blows owing to the amount of twist you get in
the mainsail (see Figures 21 and 22).

Diamond rigging

Now we come to the systems using diamond rigging. This, to
my mind, is the most effective way of stiffening a mast in any direction. I know that it is generally considered that it only restricts the
mast athwartships, but this is not true, it has considerable effect in
the fore-and-aft direction also. The reason for this is that as the centre
of the mast tries to bend forward the spreaders, which are fixed, take
the wire attached to their ends forward, whilst the side loading on the
mast is trying to force the wire to come straight. In doing this it has
the effect of pulling aft on the end of the diamond spreader and this
stiffens the mast.

Adjustable diamonds

There has been a tendency recently to have the ends of the diamond wires led on to adjustable attachment points, such as drum winches or levers, so that tension can be adjusted. I think, however, that in spite of these devices this type of rigging is too rigid and it does not give the mast sufficient chance to flex as it should in relation to the wind and sea.

Angled diamond struts

Another recent innovation is commonly known as 'forward facing diamonds'. These are diamond struts placed in the same vertical position as the original diamonds, but angled forward at some twenty degrees. They are far more effective for controlling the bend of the mast than the original diamond arrangement, and combined with a fitting which allows the diamond wire to be adjusted, they have proved to be quite successful. There are some snags, one of these is that there is really nothing to stop the mast 'popping' back in the middle when on a run. The only way to get over this is to fix the mast on the after side, at deck level and ensure that the boom is never out too far when on a run, so that there is always a certain amount of pressure on the gooseneck.

Spreader position

The vertical position of the spreader bracket is critical, and with a mast of very light section it is not always too easy to determine this position without first experimenting.

One can safely say that with keel-stepped masts that are held rigidly at deck level the spreader should be positioned just above halfway between the deck and the jib halyard sheave. With the deck-stepped mast it is just fractionally below the halfway mark.

Leach tension

In the dinghy classes, where the leach tension of the mainsail plays such an important part, experiments have been made with various types of bendy booms. This has gradually 'caught on' in the ocean racers that have mast head rigs.

Backstay

It is only recently that keel boats, using three-quarter rigs and standing backstay, found that it is an advantage to have a sail with a moderately hard leach and adjust the tension of this by the backstay. This backstay should be attached to the top of the mast at the highest point, and if that is not far enough to clear the leach of the mainsail, then a small crane can be fitted projecting aft from the top of the mast. At the stern of the boat it should run through a block or sheave situated in the deck, to some means of adjusting the tension. This can either be a tackle, a threaded mechanism, or even an easily adjustable lever, and there should be some means of recording the tension on this stay.

Runners

Runners are used on various boats, such as Stars and Dragons, and are very necessary, but again the tension on these should be easily adjusted. Unlike the other stays on the mast, they have to be easily and quickly released or tightened up, whichever the case may be. How to do so efficiently with the minimum amount of effort has been a problem. I think the answer is to have this attached to one of the stronger types of mainsheet traveller and to run it fore and aft down the side deck. Fit an adjustable stop on the traveller track so that when you pull the traveller wire aft (by some simple method such as a single length of line through a jamming cleat) it will eventually come up against the stop. By moving the traveller fore and aft along the track it should be possible to adjust the tension to a very fine degree. One could even have a length of shockcord on the forward side of the traveller so that when you let the line that is holding it back go, it would automatically run forward. This is merely an idea, but it is possible that it could be the answer to this problem.

Shroud position

The fore-and-aft position of shrouds at deck level plays an important part in the bending of the mast. With three-quarter rig I personally prefer to have the shrouds far enough aft to hold the forestay reasonably tight without putting undue compression on the mast itself, and without being too far aft to stop the boom going off when on a dead run. How far this is depends on the class of boat you are sailing. In dinghies, which have no standing backstay, I suggest the minimum would be fourteen inches (355 mm.) back from the aft side of the mast.

With keel boats that have lowers they should be exactly opposite, or even forward, of the mast so that when the mast bends the lower shrouds can stay at the same tension without restricting the mast bend.

Jumper stays

Jumper stays are still fitted to boats that have a very tall and unsupported topmast, such as the Fourteen Foot International. They are very necessary here, because otherwise the large roach that the International 14 carries on its mainsail will not stand up properly, and therefore becomes ineffective. If you do have jumpers then try to bring the ends down inside the mast from their lower attachment points to a lever, so that the tension can be adjusted. In this way it is possible to get the right setting according to the wind strength.

Two sets of spreaders

This is a new development that is intended to enable people to sail with lighter and smaller masts without appreciably increasing the windage. This is done by using two sets of limited swing spreaders, both attached to the single pair of shrouds and both individually adjustable. These two spreaders are fitted just above and below the standard positions for conventional spreaders, thereby reducing the length of unsupported mast section. Each of them is adjustable in length and angle and it should be easier to get the correct amount of mast bend. You will even be able to alter the position of the point of bend. These spreaders will have to be aerofoil in section so that they cut down on turbulence, but the overall gain over the standard type of mast with single spreader rig could be considerable.

Straightening a mast

Do not despair if you are unfortunate enough to bend an aluminium mast at any time. As long as the wall of the section is not dented it is possible to straighten it out again. This can be done by placing the mast, with the bend uppermost, across two trestles situated approximately eight feet apart (2.5 m.). Make sure these trestles are padded well. Do not attempt to straighten a mast by bending it backwards over a single trestle. This will immediately collapse the wall section and you will ruin your mast. Position the padded trestles carefully and get a couple of friends to help you balance the mast against the bend. It is no good just pressing on it, you have literally to bounce very hard four or five times. This will reduce the bend and it is just a matter then of repeating the exercise several times until the mast is straight. If you try to straighten it all in one go you could overdo it and have to start again from the other side . . . so beware! Sight along it after every four or five bounces. Masts that have been straightened this way suffer no after effects at all.

Figure 23

Halyards jumping out of luff groove

Many people have trouble with their halyards jumping out of the luff rope groove when the mast bends. This is easy enough to rectify. Arm yourself with a wooden mallet and a piece of wire the same diameter as the main halyard. Lay the mast on its back with the groove uppermost, preferably on a lawn. Close the track with the wooden mallet until the piece of wire just fails to enter the groove. (If you overdo it, it is easy enough to open it up again with a screwdriver or tyre lever.) The idea is that if the piece of wire will not come out when the sail is not in the mast, then it certainly cannot once the mainsail is also in the groove. You may well find that this has to be done every eighteen months because the continual flexing of the mast causes the luff rope groove to open.

Plate 22. Heads down! That boom is coming over with a bang. From the outline of the mainsheet it is obvious the camera has caught this 'chinese' gybe at about the time the boom was in the middle of the boat. The boom has nearly fouled the backstay which would have broken the mast. The boom vang should have been tighter.

Top: Frank Chap

Plates 23 and 24. These two pictures show great contrast in the smoothness of the set of the sails. Part of the trouble with the 14-footers in the top picture is that hardly any of them have enough tension on the luffs of their mainsails. The leach creasing is largely due to the excessive roach that these boats have to carry.

10. Booms

Types—outhauls—bendy booms—stiff booms—fittings

It is a fact that only a few years ago there were very few breakages amongst booms, and this is probably because they were large and heavy with very generous fittings. All they did was to hold out the foot of the mainsail and act as somewhere to attach the mainsheet and kicking strap. Once again recent developments in sailing have changed all this, much to the disgust of a few insurance companies whose Marine Departments are still operating on pre-war policies!

The racing boom as it is today is a refined piece of equipment which, not only does the same work as its predecessor, but can also have a pre-determined bend built into it, controls the foot tension of the mainsail, has adjustable kicking strap attachments, adjustable mainsheet attachments, sliding fittings to enable the spinnaker sheet to be pulled out to the end, the outhaul gear built inside, and it is of minimum strength and minimum weight. Usually there are two booms to every boat, one stiff and one bendy. Surely this is an incredible advance in seven years.

Types

Let us start at the beginning. It was first found that by altering the tension on the foot of the mainsail one could radically alter the shape of the sail. Slackening off the foot made the sails much fuller, and in doing so made the battens poke up to windward. This meant that the sail was far more efficient in very light weather. By doing the complete opposite, tightening up the foot of the sail, one could make the sail extremely flat and allow the end of the battens to sag off to leeward in heavy weather. This was a great advantage, since up till then it was a case of having two mainsails, one for heavy and one for light weather. You can bet that whichever one went up it was the wrong one!

Outhauls

With this new outhaul system you can have just one mainsail for any type of weather, but the foot tension has to be easily adjustable. This was done at first by taking the wire from the after end of one side of the boom, through the cringle of the mainsail and back to a small sheave on the opposite side of the boom and forward again to a cleat. This gave a two-to-one purchase, and on normal-size dinghies this was ample, until somebody discovered that even in heavy weather it paid to ease off the foot so that the mainsail became very baggy when off the wind. The problem with this was that there was just not enough purchase in the outhaul to enable you to pull the mainsail out against the tension on the leach, which was caused by a tight kicking strap. Quite often while trying to pull out the foot, the sail track on the wooden boom would split and allow the foot rope to come out for the last two feet of the groove.

It was then that metal booms came into their own. Not only were the sail track grooves much stronger, but the booms were hollow and had enough room inside to put a four-part purchase for the outhaul and for the hauling part of the tackle to come out at the forward end of the boom. This was an ideal method because it removed all the fittings and rope from the side of the boom and reduced windage and turbulence.

It was then that it was discovered that centre mainsheets were proving to be much more efficient than the old transom method, and an attachment was produced to fasten the mainsheet to the centre of the boom. At first it was one simple eye which was positioned over the point in the boat where the centre mainsheet was fixed. This was not really satifactory as it put a point loading on the boom which, although it could be made strong enough, tended to make it kink at this point.

The next modification was the track which was riveted on to the underside of the boom. In it were two slides and the mainsheet was taken through two blocks, each attached to a slide. The slides could be positioned in the track over a fairly large range. The advantage was that if you moved the slides:

1. You could close them together make the boom bend more than if they were separated.
2. You could make the boom bend evenly.
3. It allowed you to alter the angle of the mainsheet, and so made it possible to regulate the amount of bend in the mast.

Bendy booms

It was then found out that bendy booms were a distinct advantage in heavy weather. Presumably because the bend in the boom took out a certain amount of fullness in the mainsail and slackened off the leach. Although the standard booms did this to a small extent it was not considered enough.

The first bendy dinghy boom was brought out in early 1967, and it was designed to bend six inches in nine foot six inches (16 cm. in 300), which it did remarkably well. It was also very light and had the track extruded on the underside. This was full length, which allowed the kicking strap attachment to be put on to a slide, and the mainsheet attachment also, without having any track riveted on to cause weakness where the rivet holes were drilled (see Figures 24, 25, and 26).

I sailed with this type of boom for the whole of 1967 and found it highly effective in everything but the lightest of airs. Unfortunately, not all those using them had the same success and it was a long time before I found out why. It seems now that the trouble occurred when they ordered new mainsails. They worked out how much the boom was going to bend and gave this measurement to the sailmaker, who naturally built in this extra amount of flow to the bottom of the mainsail. The idea that the bendy boom takes out the flow in the middle of the mainsail will only work if it is cut to fit a straight boom. All sailmakers build a little bit of round into the mainsail foot, but if they increase this then the bendy boom has to bend twice as much before it flattens the sail. Take warning—if you have a bendy boom, do not tell the sailmaker when you order a new mainsail!

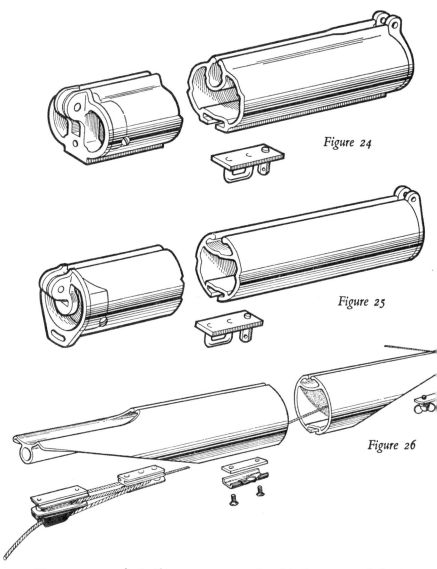

Figure 24

Figure 25

Figure 26

Figures 24, 25 and 26. Above are two examples of the latest types of alloy boom extrusions. Both have internal clew outhaul gear and integral top and bottom tracks. The upper section is designed to be flexible vertically and stiff sideways. In the middle is the specially stiff section for light weather. The lower drawing shows how the various attachments can be made to fit into the lower track. They are: the clew outhaul tackle and cleat; the kicking strap slot; and a boom take-off slide.

Fittings

Because of the track the full length of the underside of the boom, it was now possible to adjust the position of the kicking strap so that one could have it right forward in light weather and still be effective. When it blew hard it could be moved right aft. I know many Flying Dutchmen with this system that use this device for tensioning the kicking strap instead of using the usual winch on the bottom of the mast. This seemed all right up to a point, but it was very difficult to operate if you were on a run or a reach, since you could never then get the kicking strap tight.

The next gadget to appear was a small hook which slid in the track aft of the mainsheet take-off slides. This unnamed hook was for keeping the spinnaker sheets out towards the end of the boom where they did most good. It was also very good for holding the spinnaker sheet up out of the water in light weather.

Some people have elaborated this system by having a small sheave positioned on the underside of the boom, right on the outboard end, with a very thin piece of cat-gut running round it. One end is attached to the hook and the other end runs inside the boom forward. When the spinnaker sheet is put in this hook the crew pulls the hook right out to the end of the boom, giving far greater angle to the base of the spinnaker and spreading the foot of the sail effectively.

Stiff booms

Whilst racing *Shadow* during 1968, it was noticed that many boats which had the old fashioned semi-stiff boom were going fast in winds of Force 3 and less. It was also noticed that the crews were hanging out earlier and harder than in the boats with the bendy booms. It was decided then that *Shadow* would have to have another boom to see what difference it made. An extra stiff boom was manufactured from a short length of mast section and this immediately proved a huge success. Rodney Pattisson had an identical spar in his record-breaking year of 1968.

As soon as it was realised just how important it was to have a stiff boom in light weather Proctors brought out a stiff boom to match their bendy one. Nearly round in section, this boom was very light, very stiff and had the internal track on the underside, the same as on the bendy boom. This enabled each dinghy to have two booms which could be quickly interchangeable, simply by sliding the attachments from one boom to another.

I said just now that stiff booms can be used in Force 3 and under and this is, of course, an average figure with an average crew weight. Should your crew weight be high then the stiff boom can be carried in much stronger winds, but please remember that stiff booms in these conditions put more strain on the mast than a bendy boom. I suggest, if you intend to sail in this way, that you increase the stiffness of your mast. It is probably safe to say that in average wind conditions, with a light and bendy mast you should use a light and bendy boom, and with a heavy and stiff mast vice versa.

If you are unfortunate enough still to be sailing with a transom mainsheet, you will never need to use the bendy type of boom, as it will certainly bend the wrong way and make your sail fuller as the wind increases. I suggest you stick to the stiff boom, or even better, use a plank boom and if this plank boom can be induced to bend sideways, in the middle, I think you will find your boat speed improves enormously.

In small keel boats like the Tempest and the Soling, backstays are taking the place of bendy booms. In these classes it is now possible to use only the stiff boom and when the wind increases to tighten the backstay. This makes the mast bend a little more and causes your leach to slacken off, which is nearly the same as the effect of the bendy boom although you do not reduce the amount of fullness in the middle of the sail. I look forward to the day when someone will produce a simple and effective adjustable bending boom. From the way things are going I do not think it will be very long.

11. Standing and Running Rigging

Types—windage—weights—attachments

One aspect of the boat for which there can be no short cut is the standing rigging. This must be made up from the very best materials and equipment that is available. Unfortunately, it is always the most expensive.

There are only three types of standing rigging of use for a racing boat. The first is the one-by-nineteen stainless steel, second is the round rod rigging, and the third and much the best, is the lenticular (streamlined) rigging.

One-by-nineteen wire

Starting with the one-by-nineteen, this is the most common rigging and is fitted to a vast number of boats. It can have a variety of end attachments, such as the Talurit splice, which is a copper ferrule clamped around the wire after this has been bent round a thimble. A special hydraulic press is used for making this. It is worth pointing out that under no circumstances should alloy ferrules be used on stainless steel wire as a certain amount of corrosion will occur and eventually the ferrule will be split.

Terminals

The nicest and most efficient attachment is the swaged terminal. It can be obtained with either an eye, a fork or a screw-threaded

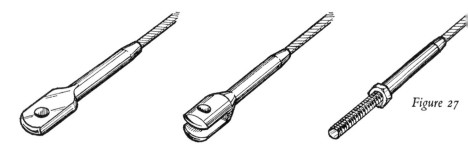

Figure 27

terminal which will enter a bottle screw. These swaged terminals are, I feel, the best method of attaching rigging. They are very small, very light and exceedingly strong, but can only be fitted with a proper swaging machine. For those who would like to put on their own terminals Norseman manufacture various types of terminals which can be clamped on to the end of the wire. It is not a very complicated procedure and the final locking is done with a spanner. The only criticism I have with this is that they tend to be slightly bulky. They make an ideal standby in your toolbox. You may need to shorten your wire, or fit a new one at some championship meeting miles away from any chandlery (and it always happens on a Sunday). Make sure if you do them yourself that you follow the instructions implicitly.

Rod rigging

The solid rod rigging is not easy to fit yourself. If you have to, the only way is as in Figure 28. Put one end through a ferrule, bend it round a thimble, push back through, and bend back the end of the rod. This is amply strong enough, but is unsightly and creates unnecessary windage and turbulence. If the rod rigging is to have the end terminals put on properly they should be screw threaded, using a

Figure 28

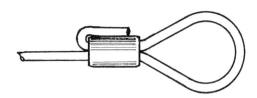

special die, or swaged. I am not absolutely convinced about round rod rigging, since there seems to be only a very small advantage over the one-by-nineteen construction. Admittedly it is smoother on the outside, but because it is round it still causes considerable drag. It is certainly more susceptible to kinking and if there is a flaw in it the whole lot will break, whereas with the one-by-nineteen just one strand will go which gives you ample warning.

Lenticular rigging

If you really want the ultimate then use lenticular (streamlined) rigging. This is a little more expensive and it takes a fair while to fit. I would suggest that you sail with standard one-by-nineteen to get your correct mast rake before fitting lenticular wires. Having tuned the boat, you can then take the exact length from the old rigging because the lenticular rigging has to be supplied to you in exact lengths complete with threaded ends.

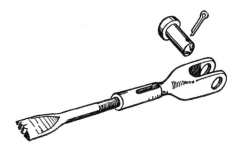

Figure 29. Lenticular rod rigging which is screw threaded and fits a standard end fitting.

There is only one snag with this type of rigging, and that is where it goes over the spreader. Because it is of solid construction it does not take too kindly to continually being straightened and bent, which is unavoidable when attached to the end of an average dinghy spreader, remembering that the dinghy spreader works part of the time in compression and part in tension. This can be avoided by asking for the part of the streamlined (lenticular) rigging, where it goes over the end of the spreader, to be made round. The manufacturers can do this, and I feel it would get over the problem. What would be ideal is if a manufacturer produced small plastic fairings that could slide over your one-by-nineteen shrouds to make them streamlined. Norseman Ropes have a fairing of this type, but it only fits larger wires and is useless for dinghies and small keel boats. They did tell me at the 1969 Boat Show that they were going to produce a small section, but nothing as yet has happened.

Shroud rollers

Quite often with large overlapping foresails you will need shroud rollers. These rollers make tacking very much easier and quicker, although they do increase the windage and turbulence. Below you will see a diagram (Figure 30) of a shroud roller which I consider is ideal and which reduces wind resistance to the minimum.

Figure 30

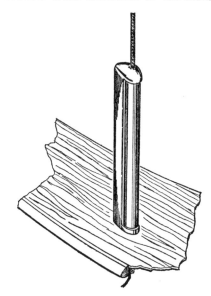

Shackles

Never use shackles when fastening standing rigging. There are more cases of mast breakage where shackles have been used than from any other cause. If you must use something, then use a toggle which has been specially designed and tested for the job.

It is difficult to recommend the exact size of rigging to be used for any boat. It is well known that 75 per cent of the classes racing today have rigging that is much stronger than required. I cannot help feeling that this is a good thing. It gives a much higher safety factor at clevis pins, swages, etc. Also, if you are in collision or your crew falls against the shroud, injury is less likely because the rigging is much bigger. A good example of what I mean is the old-fashioned method of cutting cheese which was always done with a very thin wire. Imagine what fine wire could do to cold, wet hands if someone fell against it. On the whole I am in favour of the slightly heavier rigging.

I have always liked to use galvanised, flexible wire for running rigging as this has given me plenty of warning when it intends to break, simply by going rusty, whereas the stainless steel wire breaks when you least expect it and without much warning.

Main halyard

Main halyards should be a size larger than was used six or seven years ago. This is because the cunningham hole system puts a very much greater strain on the halyard. When fastening the main halyard (and I have mentioned this before) it should go on to some type of hook rack, rather than a cleat, to keep the stretch to the minimum. If there is a large eye splice on the bottom of the halyard you can knot the rope tail to it, and by undoing it when the mainsail is up you will be able to stow this halyard away somewhere, or even use it as the anchor warp.

Jib halyard

The same goes for the jib halyard, and again this should be a little on the heavy side, especially if you are using a furling gear.

Furling gear

Incidentally when using the furling gear make sure it revolves the right way, i.e. when rolling the sail up it should turn the wire against its lay. If it does not, and turns the opposite way, then breakage in the jib halyard will occur. The easy way to work this out is that when you are looking down on the furling gear it should turn clockwise to wind up the sail (see Figure 31).

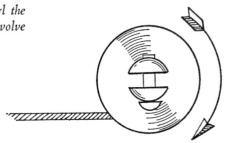

Figure 31. Pull on the line to furl the jib and the drum should revolve clockwise.

All boats have trouble with their forestays when using a furling gear, especially at the top where the swivel catches on the loose forestay and winds it up into the sail. One way of stopping this is by putting a small disc on your top swivel, which should be at least three inches (76 mm) in diameter. When you roll the jib up the swivel will go round, and so will the disc, but it will also keep the forestay a reasonable distance away. This is a much neater method than many I have seen, which use great thick lumps of shockcord taken from the forestay up to the spinnaker crane, making the whole area round the hounds look like a jungle.

Points to watch

This is a good place to point out that although you might use rigging that is slightly heavier than is actually needed, make sure everything is neat. All the split pins should point the right way and there should be no loose pieces of tape to come undone. Always make sure that what you have aboard is absolutely essential, if it is not, throw it away. Many masts are being used today with shrouds hung on to a bolt running through the mast, which has a head on one end, and a nut on the other. Please get rid of this. It does no good at all and so replace it with a belled-out tube. The lips of the tube can be faired in with a plastic filler so making the whole of this area smooth. This levelling and fairing of ridges with a filler is very important and it should be done where there are any rivet heads or spreader fittings. Make sure that the spreader does not stick out beyond the end of the shroud. If it does, cut it off. Remove all tape and wiring from the end of the spreaders and see if there is some other way that you can lock it in. Usually, this can be done by putting a small length of wire round the shroud, taking this wire back inside the spreader and locking it at the inboard end.

Sheets

Sheets have to be a personal preference. It would seem that the most suitable type of rope is the plaited terylene with a matt finish, not the shiny one. I prefer the sixteen plait, as it has more body and is less likely to flatten where it goes round sheaves or in cleats. The soakage rate is not as great either. One thing I have noticed in most boats I have borrowed is that the jib sheets, main sheets and spinnaker sheets are always far longer than is really necessary. Next time you have your boat rigged on the shore try pushing the boom out against the shroud. If you have a centre mainsheet on a traveller, push the traveller out with it and see how much mainsheet you have over that could be cut off. After all, this unused length of rope does nothing more than soak up water, increase the weight, and tangle with everything it comes in contact with. I would not mind taking a bet that you can get rid of ten to fifteen feet of rope from your boat if you try.

12. *Spinnaker Equipment*

Spinnaker boom, type, weight, and fittings—spinnaker boom uphaul and downhaul—spinnaker sheet and halyard attachments—spinnaker sheets—spinnaker bags and turtles—spinnaker chutes

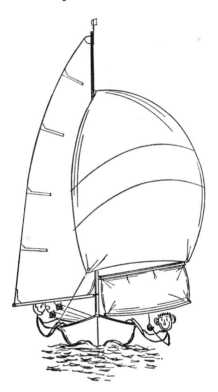

Figure 32

Spinnaker equipment and spinnaker handling are amongst the most controversial subjects ever discussed at the club bar. Everybody has his own pet method, which usually entails having umpteen different makes of equipment. Personally, I do not think it matters which system you use, as long as it is laid out efficiently and simply.

Spinnaker boom

The first item you will need is a spinnaker boom. Unlike the other spars on the boat this does not have to be small (unless stowed on the foredeck), as it usually is in a Soling or a Dragon, but it does have to be light. The reason that size does not matter being that it is always set with the wind either abeam or right aft so that windage, instead of being a disadvantage, becomes just the opposite. (I have thought about having a roller blind set into the spinnaker boom, so that when on a run you just pulled it out! (Figure 32). There is normally no rule against this as there is no maximum diameter for the spinnaker pole in any class.) The weight, however, is important. Whether or not the boom is stowed on deck or inside the hull, it must be light. This helps to reduce the all-up weight of your boat, and also makes the boom easier to handle.

The type of fitting you put on the end of the spinnaker pole is just a matter of personal preference again. I think I can safely say that the ideal spinnaker pole end has not yet been designed. A sweeping statement you might think, but I doubt it. The type of end needed should be small in overall size and light in weight, but with a large opening between the jaws. The plunger should be able to be locked open until released by a trigger; to open it you should either pull a string or squeeze a trigger mounted in the tube. The present method of opening many existing fittings is to pull on the plunger with the thumb. This is not good, since it is very difficult for a right-handed person to operate left handed. Even worse, if you are standing on the foredeck with the spinnaker pole right above you, I would say it was virtually impossible. With a trigger on the tubing itself, all you would have to do would be to squeeze, and it would not matter being left handed, right handed, underneath or above it, the jaws could still easily be opened. I would not be surprised if such a fitting was with us in three years or so; though it would be a difficult design problem.

Spinnaker boom uphaul and downhaul

Once you have obtained a boom with some decent end fittings (I can recommend ones like those illustrated here), the next point is the means by which you hold the spinnaker boom horizontal, i.e.

Figure 33. A typical good, simple end fitting showing the rounded shape necessary for the free running of the guy.

the uphaul and the downhaul. The most popular method in dinghies is to use a shockcord lift, and an adjustable rope downhaul. These two are joined together, and the top end of the shockcord is made fast to a small eye mounted on the mast in the region of the spreaders. If you have no spreaders, then put it approximately halfway up the mast to the hounds. The rope downhaul goes through a fairlead to a small jam cleat, situated just forward of the mast at deck level. At the top end of the rope part of the system, just where it joins the shockcord, there should be a series of knots. They should number approximately five, and should be two inches apart. On the spinnaker boom, in the centre and on either side, should be a small special nylon cleat. The arms of this cleat are arranged so that they are both pointing inwards. One of the best on the market at present is made by Holt-Allen (see Figure 34).

When setting the spinnaker, your crew attaches the outboard end of the spinnaker boom into the tack, grabs hold of the uphaul and downhaul at the point where the knots are, and inserts the rope between one pair of knots into the Holt-Allen cleat. When this is done he then pushes the spinnaker boom right out to its full extent and clips it on to the mast. The final adjustment is the tightening up of the downhaul (Figure 35).

The idea of having the knots is so that should any slip occur in the jam cleat, the knots will come up against it and stop the rope going any further. There are some snags with this system: one is that the

Figure 34. A good type of spinnaker boom cleat for small dinghies.

Plate 25. A spinnaker boom end fitting which opens by squeezing the plunger. This makes it particularly easy to operate. There is also a rope running down through the tube and up to the inner side of the squeeze-plate so that it can be operated from the other end if required.

Plate 26. The windage and weight of a spinnaker boom track can be saved by replacing it with a sliding saddle. Shaped to the section of the mast it is usually lined with P.T.F.E. to reduce friction to a minimum.

spinnaker boom is not rigidly held in the horizontal position, the outboard end can still move up and down about three inches, owing to the boom twisting due to slop in the mast connection, which causes the Holt-Allen cleat position on the side of the boom, to vary from being on top to underneath. Secondly, there are a lot of projections in front of the mast, causing increased turbulence; and thirdly, when you end-to-end the pole for gybing, nine times out of ten the rope slips out of the centre jamb cleat, letting the pole go skywards. Then you have to start all over again.

Figure 35. The arrangement of a spinnaker boom on a dinghy.

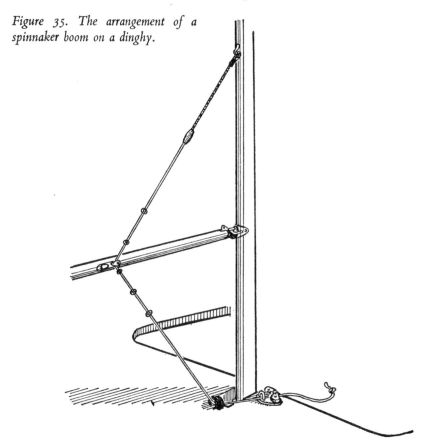

The method I used in *Shadow*, which was devised and operated by David Hunt, was incredibly good; but before I describe this, please remember that David is six foot five inches tall. He started by leading the uphaul to the inside of the spinnaker boom. This was done by drilling a hole in the centre of the boom, on top, and putting a fairing piece in the hole to stop the uphaul chafing. Inside the pole was a length of shockcord running to one end. The tension on this cord could be adjusted, since it was passed through a hole at the end of the tube with a knot on the outside. It was just a matter of tightening it up and putting the knot in a different place. The uphaul then ran down through the hole in the centre of the spinnaker boom, through a block attached to the shockcord and back to the opposite end, where it came out at the side of the boom twelve inches (30 cm.) from the end. On the end of this line was a small hook which could be hitched into a number of holes drilled in the end of the boom, at approximately one inch centres (see Figure 36).

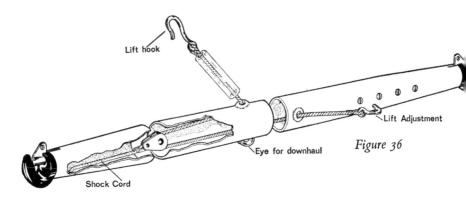

Lift hook

Lift Adjustment

Eye for downhaul

Figure 36

Shock Cord

At a quick glance, the whole thing looked rather like a flute. On the end of the uphaul was fastened a small hook which, when the spinnaker boom was in position, was connected to an eye on the front of the mast exactly two feet (60 cm.) above the eye to which the inner end of the spinnaker boom was fastened.

On the underside of the spinnaker boom, in the middle, was fitted a small stainless steel eye. On to this eye was hooked the downhaul, which then led through the deck approximately six inches (15 cm.) forward of the mast, down and via a sheave on the hog or spine, back to a jamb cleat. Between the deck and the sheave on the hog, the downhaul was passed through a small block, to which was attached a length of shockcord, which ran up to the bow. The idea of the shockcord was that when you unhooked the downhaul from the spinnaker pole the tension was taken off it. The shockcord then pulled the downhaul back up forward under the deck, until the hook came down and stowed into its hole. When it was required it was a simple matter of catching hold of the hook and pulling it out from the deck to hook on the pole. We used this system for some three years without trouble.

One disadvantage with our method was that first you had to clip on the downhaul, and then clip the uphaul to the mast before fitting the spinnaker pole to either the sail or the mast, making an extra operation, whereas with the simple system of shockcord and knots, all that was needed was to clip it into the centre cleat in one movement. I think, though, that the advantages gained from our system outweighed the disadvantages. There was no shockcord permanently fixed on the front of the mast; the downhaul and uphaul were self-stowing; and when you gybed you could be sure it could be done with perfect safety and control, because there was nothing to come undone. Many times we were able to gybe inside the boat ahead at the wing mark on the Olympic course, and got away with it because we had this foolproof system.

Attaching spinnaker halyards and sheets

Fastening the sheets and halyards to the spinnaker is always a problem. Troubles arise with just about all the fittings available today, and many people have gone back to the old-fashioned method of simply tying a knot. One trouble seems to be that some fittings are not strong enough, which is certainly the case with clip hooks made from aluminium, but if they were not made from this material they would be too heavy. Another problem comes with the very small snap shackles, where the head of the plunger is so large that it is liable to catch in everything, and instantly releases the spinnaker.

On the whole I think that snap shackles are the best answer; but they do need some modification before use. Try using a small half-round file on either side of the head of the plunger until it is filed away flush with the main body. When this is done if you wish to open it, it is possible to twist the plunger so that the unfiled part of the head is projecting, pull back the plunger and fix the snap shackle to the spinnaker. If the plunger head is turned back so that it is in line with the body nothing can catch on it (see Figure 37).

Figure 37

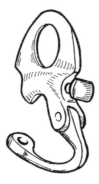

Do remember to have the smallest diameter spinnaker sheets that you can handle in comfort, and do not have them too long. With the spinnaker stowed in its basket, a sheet of the correct length should reach from the basket, round the forestay, back around the outside of the boat, through the sheave at the after end and back amidships again. Do not forget to make the other sheet exactly the same length! If you have carried out my earlier suggestions, and have the sheets running from the after sheave underneath the deck and coming out into the cockpit amidships, it is valuable to join the two sheets together, which avoids some of the possible snarl-ups.

Presumably you will measure up your sheets whilst on shore. Another job to tackle at the same time is the positioning of your sheets for the gybe. With a dinghy, you can turn the boat around on the trailer until the wind is dead astern and set your spinnaker exactly as though you were sailing. Set the two clews at equal distance from the stern in such a position that if you had two spinnaker poles they would be at forty-five degrees to the centreline. Having done this, mark the spinnaker sheets at the point where they are cleated with black paint. There is a great advantage in having these marks, especially for heavy weather. Imagine you are running and are about to gybe. All you need to do is to cleat both sheets and guy on the marks, safe in the knowledge that, when you gybe, the spinnaker will stay set and be exactly right for the new tack.

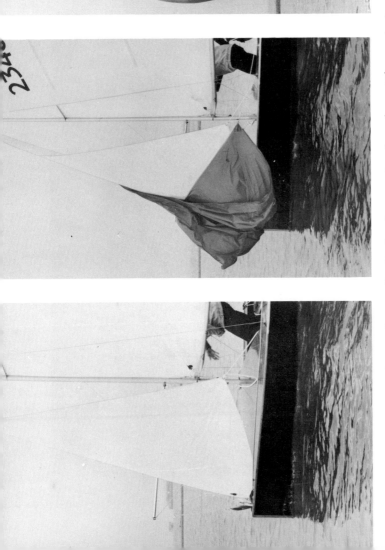

Plates 27, 28 and 29. This Merlin–Rocket has a spinnaker chute. The retrieving line can be seen leading from just below the centre of the spinnaker, forward and down through a chute at the stem. In the centre picture the sheet and guy are held tight whilst the spinnaker is drawn into the chute. The left-hand picture shows the spinnaker fully stowed with the three ends just showing from the top of the chute.

Plate 31. An ordinary aluminium washing-line winder contains the spinnaker halyard. The surplus halyard is wound

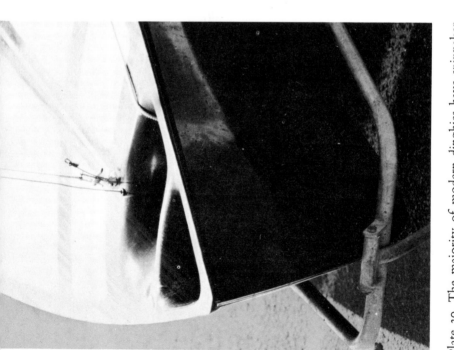

Plate 30. The majority of modern dinghies have spinnaker chutes but here is one that has two, one for a reaching spin-

Light-weather spinnaker sheets

You should carry in the boat one length of thin polypropylene line to use as a light-weather spinnaker sheet. It does really make a great deal of difference to the set of the spinnaker in very light airs, by getting rid of the normal heavier sheets. During the 1967 F.D. World Championship in Montreal, where for five days there was hardly any wind at all, I remember reaching down one leg of the course without any sheets on the spinnaker at all, just relying on the weight of the cloth itself to keep the spinnaker in the right position, and this it did beautifully as long as the boat was held steady. In this sort of conditions the guy does not matter too much, as the weight is taken by the uphaul and downhaul on the boom. Although, if you gybe, you will have to do a quick swop round.

Spinnaker halyard swivels

There is a swivel on most of the spinnakers made today, but since I have broken every one of these swivels that I have ever had I now treat them with great suspicion, taking them off immediately I receive the new sail. The best swivel I have ever found can be purchased from any deep-water fishing shop. It is no more than three-quarters of an inch (19 mm.) long and is tested to 600 pounds (275 kg.) breaking strain, and believe it or not . . . costs only 30 new pence. One of these days I intend putting one of these swivels on to each of the clews as well, so that, if the clews get twisted before you put it on to the spinnaker boom end they will untwist themselves. You will not have this problem if you attach the spinnaker boom to the guy itself, because if there is any twist in the spinnaker at this time the rope will allow the twist to come out. It is very useful using this system if you have a spinnaker chute, as you can haul the spinnaker down into the chute, and if you let the guy run through the end of the spinnaker pole it saves rushing.

The spinnaker halyard should have a mark on it at the bottom (where you jam it) to ensure that the head of the spinnaker never comes closer than twelve to eighteen inches (30–45 cm.) from the mast. This is advisable in all conditions except very heavy weather, when it is worth pulling the spinnaker hard into the mast to reduce any rolling effect that a slack halyard may induce.

There are many ways of hoisting and lowering a spinnaker, and a few golden rules should always be kept: such as, whenever possible setting a spinnaker to leeward, never sheeting in before the guy has been cleated, and never sheeting in before the spinnaker has been fully hoisted; when lowering never try to lower a full sail, always let one end or the other go, and hold one edge tightly so that the sail just flaps. If the sail does get into trouble by falling in the water, remember there will be little weight left in it if you can let one corner go.

Spinnaker stowage

Stowage of spinnakers varies with each class of boat. In dinghies spinnaker bags are let into the forward deck. When the spinnaker is lowered it can be guided straight down into this bag, so that it is instantly ready for resetting again.

In keel boats, because of its size, the spinnaker usually has to come down in the lee of the mainsail, straight into the cockpit. Once you have it down and have removed the sheets and halyard, it has to be bagged, and the easiest way of doing this is start at the head with a person on each leach coiling it up, when they reach the foot it is possible to let go and bag the rest of the spinnaker, the coiled leaches going in last.

Most spinnaker bags are called turtles and they have two uses. First, they can be used to bag the sail as described, and secondly they can be used when hoisting the sail. This is done by taking it forward and strapping on to the foredeck, complete with halyard guy and sheet. When rounding the windward mark it is then a simple matter to pull the halyard and the fastening holding the top of the bag, which may be just a light line or Velcro, will break open and the spinnaker emerge.

It is for this reason that most of the spinnaker bags, or turtles, have a flat wooden base so that they either lay flat on the foredeck or fit against the forward side of the forestay. It is a long-winded method to send a crew up forward to lash this on the bow, and it also upsets the balance of the boat enormously. I only hope that it will soon be possible to fit spinnaker chutes to all classes of boat.

A chute is really a fabulous way of stowing the spinnaker. Not only can you stow it without going right forward, but it can be done so quickly and neatly that when it is stowed it is ready for instant rehoisting.

The entrance to the chute must be perfect to avoid friction, and must also be the correct aperture for the size of the spinnaker you intend using. As I have mentioned before, these chutes can be obtained from leading boat-builders. Bob Hoare of Christchurch makes a very good one for Flying Dutchmen and similar boats.

The entrance of the chute is fitted to the boat and then you have to buy a long, tapered tube of some porous material from the sailmaker. The reason this tube needs to be tapered is that as you pull the spinnaker down into it, the tapering of the tube forces out the air and the porosity is to allow this air to escape. The length of this tube depends on the size of your spinnaker, which can be calculated if you remember that the line that pulls the spinnaker back into the chute is attached to the middle of the sail. In the F.D. class the tube is approximately ten feet long.

To stow the spinnaker into the tube ready for launching one first needs a messenger line running through the chute. This messenger is then tied to the reinforced patch in the middle of the spinnaker (which, incidentally, must be put on all spinnakers that are likely to be used with chutes). The centre of the sail can then be pulled back, through the chute into the tube. When it is right inside all that will be showing from the mouth of the chute will be the two clews and the head. To these should be fastened the sheets and the halyard. Back in the cockpit, the messenger line should be removed and the other end of the spinnaker halyard fastened on instead. When this is done the spinnaker is ready for setting. If it is the first time you have used a chute, practice a few times on shore first until you get it right.

To hoist, all one does is to pull away on the halyard. Make sure that the other end of the halyard is free to run up inside the tube. As the spinnaker emerges from the chute the crew should pull hard on the guy until he can attach the pole. By the time he has the pole rigged, the helmsman should have the spinnaker hoisted and cleated, and it should be setting perfectly.

To lower the spinnaker, the crew must pull hard on the sheet and guy until the foot is pressing tightly against the luff of the jib. The helmsman should then let go of the halyard and pull in on the other end of the spinnaker halyard which passes through the chute. Because the foot of the spinnaker is tightly held it cannot drop, and the centre of the spinnaker enters the chute first. As soon as this happens the crew can let go of the guy and sheet and remove the pole. By this time the whole spinnaker should have disappeared into the great gaping hole, leaving just sheets and halyard protruding. The system is very easy to operate, but does need split-second co-operation between the helmsman and crew for maximum safety and speed.

Sailing with a spinnaker is great fun, it demands courage, team work and concentration from whoever is controlling it. As long as your gear is strong and simple, and you have confidence in it, you need never be afraid of setting it.

13. Sails

Mainsail, jib, spinnaker—shape—trimming—setting—battens—sheeting material

If only the first person to put up a reed mat as a sail on a boat knew what he had started! Books have been written about sails; fortunes have been made and lost on them, and universities have spent enormous sums in trying to find out how they work, and still we are little closer to a complete answer.

Over the years, I have read many books describing the ideal sail shape, and it seems that they are unanimous in that there is only one shape worth having. What they fail to explain is why, if you have a sail designed and cut to their ideal shape, it will make one class go very

Plate 32. The Dragon, a notoriously wet boat, must have some means of keeping the water out of the spinnaker chute. This one has a sliding hatch which opens by pulling the control line from the cockpit, and closes by means of a shock cord.

Plate 33. Windows in sails should be positioned for the maximum effect. Z 142 has one in the top of the jib so that the forward crew man can watch the luff of the spinnaker. Boats with large overlapping headsails should have windows high in the luff of the mainsail to enable the leach of the genoa to be seen.

fast, and be utterly useless on another class. The sail that makes this first class go very fast probably does not compare in any way to the ideal sail for the second class. If you expect me to tell you why this is so you will be unlucky, because I admit I am as much in the dark as anyone else. I am pleased about this though, as it enables me to go on experimenting in the hopes that one day I may be the one to find the answer.

I must say that I do not think we have progressed very far at all when it comes to sail shape. Peter Barton gave me a copy of a very old book, I should think about the first of its kind, on racing. One of the chapters in it explains how to stretch your vertical cut, gaff mainsail. First, it states, you need leather pouches and thongs equal to the number of seams in the mainsail. Along with this you would also need a considerable amount of lead shot. To quote 'to stretch your main so that it is suitable for racing one must first have a dry and sunny day with a light breeze. The main should be hoisted, so that the luff and leach are just tight, and the gaff peaked until the creases disappear from the throat. The vessel should be left at anchor with the head towards the wind, so that the main can flap gently. Stitch the leather sacks, one to each seam, approximately three feet above the boom. When this is done each sack should have a small amount of lead put in it. The amount of lead to vary according to where you want the maximum amount of flow to be. The first seam near the luff should have a quarter pound and as you work back the amount to be increased until the seam, where the maximum amount of flow should be, has two pounds in the sack. From there on to the leach it should be tailed off evenly. This sail should then be allowed to flap gently for the rest of the day. If you need a sail with more fullness the weight in the sacks should be increased.' If that is not scientific I do not know what is! Who would go to that amount of trouble to get their sails right these days? It seems to me that too many of us send our sails straight back to the sailmaker, instead of persevering.

To order a mainsail

Whilst on the subject of mainsails, when ordering this sail, give the sailmaker a chance by telling him what you want. That is, for example, that the luff should set to the black bands instead of having to be pulled. The cunningham hole eye should be situated eight to nine inches (20–23 cm.) above the tack cringle. The mainsail should have a medium amount of flow, and should be cut for a mast that bends approximately eight inches (20 cm.) between the black bands. The foot should be cut for a straight boom, and without any strain on it the clew should lie approximately two inches (50 cm.) in from the black band (this example is for the average dinghy). I do believe that I can hear the sailmakers outcry already! This is how I have ordered all my sails and I have never had a really bad one.

Fullness

If you can obtain a mainsail of average fullness it is possible, by experimenting, to induce the correct amount of flow for most conditions. It is governed by the tension on the luff, the tension on the foot, the flexibility of the battens and the amount of bend in the mast and boom. If, in medium airs, you find that you can easily hold the boat upright and that a short steep sea stops the boat, it is a sure sign that the mainsail is too flat.

To rectify this I suggest you try easing the foot of the mainsail by one inch to one and a half inches (25–40 mm.), this has to be worked in conjunction with the cunningham hole, which should not be too tight. If this still does not give the mainsail enough power, put in a more flexible top batten and tie this in, so that when the mainsail is up and setting properly it gives a reasonable amount of flow right up to the top. You may find that stiffening up the mast will help a little too. These small adjustments should give you a very powerful mainsail, but one that only the heavy weights will be able to use in medium weather, but ideally suited for light weights in lighter airs.

Once you have decided on the amount of fullness you require you must then find the correct position for the 'maximum point of fullness'. I have found that this position does depend on weather conditions, so that in heavy weather I need the fullness well forward, and in light weather well back towards the middle of the sail. The easiest way to do this is with the cunningham hole—if you tighten it up it will pull the fullness forward—slacken it and the fullness will go aft. If the mast is allowed to flex it will also push the fullness aft, but you can forget this because in doing so it tends to flatten the mainsail also.

Leach tensions

We have discussed leach tensions in another chapter, but I feel it is a subject we should go into again whilst dealing with mainsails, because leaches are very important.

Leaches on mainsails can be broken down into two categories: 'tight leach' and 'loose leach'. A tight leached mainsail is one where the ends of the battens are pointing up to windward hard, no matter what the force of wind is. This is caused by too much cloth being taken in on the very edge of the leach, compared with the seams at the inboard end of the batten. Unless you have a really bendy boom and a very flexible top mast you will find that it is very difficult, with this type of sail, to make it perform well in winds over Force 3.

A loose leached mainsail is, of course, the complete reverse. It gives the helmsman and crew the impression of being completely flat. You will find that no amount of tension on the mainsheet, and neither a stiff top mast nor a straight boom, can possibly bring the leach on to a line between the end of the boom and the top of the mast. When you are in a strong wind and you have to let the mainsail flog, instead of the front third of the mainsail lifting as is usual, the whole sail will lift from luff to leach. Remember that a tight leach will encourage weather helm, whilst a slack leach will do the opposite. Only in a very few special cases is it an advantage to have a loose leach. Usually it is better to have a mainsail somewhere between the two, and control leach tension by various methods for different wind strengths.

A tight leach in light weather is ideal, but in heavy weather it will ruin your performance. This is the reason why you should always carry two top battens on board, one bendy and one stiff. Fifteen minutes before the starting gun you will be able to change the batten if necessary to suit the weather conditions prevailing. Surprising as it may seem, a stiff top batten in light weather can alone be responsible for taking all the power out of your mainsail, and the same applies in reverse if a bendy one is used in heavy winds. This, of course, applies mainly to sails with a full width top batten. In light weather a tight leach can also be obtained simply by having a stiff boom and a tight mainsheet.

One other point to watch is the angle of the battens to the centre-line when the sail is sheeted in. Invariably, in very light weather, it seems advantageous for the battens to poke up to windward. This can be achieved, not by tightening up any more on the mainsheet, but by slackening off the foot, which allows the sail to be much fuller and brings the outboard end of the battens well up to windward of the centreline of the boat. Adjusting the tension on the foot from the inboard end via a cunningham hole on the foot has been tried, but it did not work, since it only operated on the lower half of the mainsail. If you adjust the sail from the outboard end it is possible to alter the flow over the whole area.

Built-in flow

The flow in the sails should be built in, and should not rely on the luff being 'cut round', as was the method many years ago. You can, in fact, still wander round the London Boat Show and see the odd sail cut in this fashion. They are easily identifiable, as there is a big ridge running down the luff about two or three inches from the mast. This is caused by the round having been pushed back by the straight mast. The sailmakers will argue that this ridge will come out when the wind blows. They are quite right, but unfortunately, when it does come out the fullness is too near the luff and, what happens on a calm day? Do they expect you to sail with a huge crease at the front of the sail?

To find out if your sails have a built-in fullness spread them out on the floor, stretching out all the edges until you have removed as many of the crinkles as possible. On the good sail you will find it impossible to flatten out the centre. Of course, there is always a small amount of round at the luff and the foot to accommodate mast bend, but there should always be a great deal of loose cloth in the centre and, if there is not, then send the sail back.

I once ordered a jib for a friend from a leading sailmaker. I had previously explained that the flow should be built in, and why. When he received his jib he asked me to go and look at it. Was my face red! Stretched out on his floor it looked like a sheet of linoleum. Obviously it had been cut out of a flat sheet of cloth. Needless to say, it went straight back to the sailmaker the next day.

When sailing for the first time with a new sail, choose a warm, sunny day with a light breeze. Use the sail gently, never haul it out to the black bands in the first six hours' sailing. In fact, treat it as if it

Sports Illustrated

Plate 34. There is just enough wind to get the crew out on the wire and the cunningham hole on the mainsail has yet to be pulled down. The spinnaker halyard lies across the windward side of the jib which disturbs the flow over the sails. Better to have a downhaul so that it can be kept tight in front of the jib luff. You can see from the position of the tiller that this boat is beautifully balanced and should be 'eating up to windward'.

Plate 35. An aerial view of a Tempest clearly showing the twist in the mainsail and the jib and the near parallel slot between the jib leach and the back of the mainsail which could nevertheless be improved by bringing the jib fairlead further inboard, slackening the sheet, and allowing the leach to twist off a little bit more. Note the leeway angle shown by the wake.

were a new cotton sail. The sailmakers do not think this treatment
necessary, but in the past I have found that sails treated this way have
the minimum number of creases in them. I don't know why this
should be so. It is just one of those things.

After a season's hard use you will find it considerably more difficult
to pull the sail out to the black bands. The reason is that the luff rope
is shrinking. Do not order a new sail—just send this one back to the
sailmaker to be re-roped and it will be as good as ever. After two
seasons' use the cloth itself will have shrunk too much, and then I am
afraid the only thing you can do is buy a new one.

To order a jib

One of your problems, providing, of course, you are not a Finn,
O.K., or Moth sailor, will be finding a good jib and, once having
found it, setting it correctly. Of the two working sails, I feel that the
jib is often the most neglected, except in the Flying Dutchman class,
where it is the complete opposite. As I have said before, no part of the
boat should be neglected; everything must be as perfect as it is
possible to make it.

Apart from having a choice, I see no reason to need two or three
jibs. I consider that you should stick to one jib and one only throughout the season, and that this jib should be paired to one mainsail. If
you want a change, replace them both, but not one or the other.
You should get to know each setting of the jib so that it corresponds
with the setting of the mainsail, and vice versa. If at any time you
change only one sail it will take many days racing to find the settings
again, and I do not suppose even then you will be going any faster
than originally.

As with the mainsail, when ordering a jib insist that they build in
the flow completely and do not cut the luff round. The jib is unsupported along the luff and therefore will tend to curve inwards, and
so a curve cut on to the luff will produce a jib with the flow right up
against the leading edge. Lack of drive and poor pointing ability will
be the result. It is good to have a jib which has the maximum point of
flow just over 25 per cent of its width from the luff. The lead in from
the luff to this point should be as straight as possible, with the minimum curvature (see Figure 38). The tack and head cringles should be

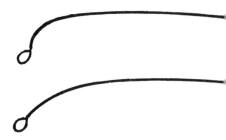

Figure 38. A sail with curvature as in the upper sketch will not be able to point as high as the one shaped as in the lower drawing, even though the maximum curvature is the same.

in the cloth and not out on a limb, as in the sketch (see Figure 39). In this way you will get maximum area in the limits allowed.

If you have a choice of design I recommend the lowest cut of jib you can fit into the boat. Make it a real deck sweeper! If you can do this and add a rounded foot as well, so that as soon as you ease the jib slightly the round of the foot drops over the gunwale, so much the better as there is a great escape of air underneath the foot of any sail (see Plate 25). If you can close this slot it forces the air to run fore and aft along the outline of the sail, giving more power. Oddly enough, with a very high-cut jib this problem does not seem to occur.

Figure 39

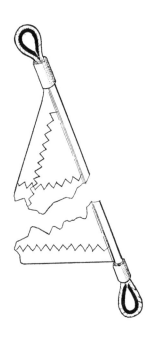

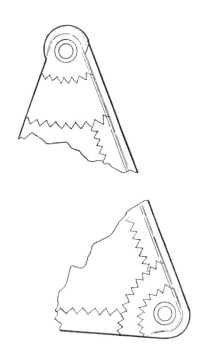

Although the air flow does escape round the lower edge, it is still flowing horizontally across the sail. It seems that this only happens when the foot is horizontal and with a gap below. I have often felt that, as in rudders, the low-cut jib is essential for open water sailing but, on small lakes and rivers, the high-cut jib can be used with advantage, mainly because the maximum area is higher up and, because of the short leach, the sail is better balanced for light weather. With a low-cut jib there is more weight of cloth in the bottom of the sail and it usually hangs dead, unless one can hold up the clew of the sail by hand.

Cunningham holes in jibs are becoming more and more popular and have come into their own with long-footed jibs, where the flow in the sail can be adjusted easily. They are not so effective in a jib with a short foot.

Sheeting angle

Sheeting angles have been played about with for years. Boats have been given wide sheeting angles and some others very narrow sheeting angles. Oddly enough, neither seems to make much difference and, like everybody else, I have a theory and for what it is worth, here it is: first of all, I do not think the sheeting angle (the angle at the base of the forestay between the centreline and the jib fairlead) is the important thing. It is the fore-and-aft position of the sheet lead which is the secret.

I suggest that you start by having the narrowest sheeting angle you can possibly fit into the boat, that is at the same time convenient. In other words, somewhere to fasten the sheet leads roughly halfway from the centreline to the outboard edge and fix them in this position. The distance is not important as long as it is not too far out. Having done this, one then ought to sail the boat hard on the wind in a reasonable breeze, the idea being to find out which lifts first, mainsail or jib. You will usually find that the mainsail will lift a long time before the jib. This is caused by the jib leach being too tight and the air that is flowing across the jib is forced into the leeward side of the mainsail, thus creating what is known as backwinding. This being so, the fairlead must be moved aft. Go on doing this until eventually both the jib and the mainsail lift together. When this happens you have gone too far and will have to move the fairleads forward a fraction, so that the mainsail lifts a little before the jib. Once you have found this spot mark it, preferably also noting the strength of the wind. If it was a Force 4, for example, you can mark the position as being Number Four. After this go out again when the wind is lighter and carry out the whole exercise again. You will find that the jib fairlead will now need to be in a different position. Again mark it up for the strength of wind.

If you have a jib with a long foot and a comparatively short leach the fairlead position for light weather should be further forward. With a jib that has a long leach and a short foot the fairlead position will be further aft. All we are really doing is adjusting the tension of the leach of the jib in various winds, and so making the correct slot between the leach and the mainsail in differing conditions. Once you have found these positions it is very simple to put your fairleads in any given place for any type of weather. Do not forget that if you change your sails you will have to start all over again.

With low-cut jibs that have a short foot try to fit the fairleads somewhere inside the boat, so that you will have at least eighteen to twenty-four inches (45–60 cm.) between the sail and the fairlead. When reaching the jib will hook in too much if you do not have this amount of scope. If this is impossible the only way to get over the problem is by having a barber hauler or a reaching hook (see Figure 5).

Ease jib sheets in light weather

Before we pass on to spinnakers, a word of advice. In light weather everybody eases the mainsheet, the outhaul, and the cunningham hole, so that the mainsail becomes full and powerful. Very few sail around with a slack jib sheet; try it some time and really give the jib a chance to pull. You will also be able to see when the jib is lifting and most important, it will stop you from pinching.

Spinnaker

Spinnaker setting and handling techniques have been pushed along rapidly by classes such as Five-O-Fives, Flying Dutchmen, and International Fourteens. Another class which is also catching up fast is the Merlin Rocket development class. It was not so long ago that spinnakers were used mainly well off the wind but now, under certain conditions, they are used for close reaching. The handling techniques vary from country to country. The latest advance in this direction is, of course, handling the spinnaker from the end of a trapeze which, in very rough weather, is far from easy.

All this has brought about a new type of spinnaker which is very light and strong, with low water absorbancy, and has a very low porosity. It is usually broad shouldered with a lot of stiffening in the head and can be set on a reach with the leading edge rolled in, so giving maximum drive without backwinding the mainsail. With the Olympic course being used everywhere nowadays, reaching with the spinnaker is very important. On the standard Olympic courses there are two reaches and one run, and you seem to lose very little when you are dead before the wind by setting a spinnaker that is designed for reaching. Probably this is because very few people sail truly dead before the wind since, when the spinnaker is set, it often pays to tack down wind. In this way you have the wind on the quarter instead of dead astern which has the effect of bringing the apparent wind further ahead, which makes the spinnaker much more efficient and, of course, increases the boat speed enormously.

I have no idea how to cut a spinnaker, but I can tell you the faults to look for. First and foremost is an unstable spinnaker, one that it is exceedingly difficult to keep filled without oversheeting it. The correctly shaped spinnaker can be sailed with a large percentage of the leading edge rolled back and the effect is rather like the lifting luff of the mainsail. It is because of this that you can get the maximum drive from the spinnaker and it is possible to sail with the sheet eased out far more, thereby letting the wind flow across the sail rather than in it and this gives far greater driving force.

When the wind drops light some spinnakers develop a crease running from the head to just below the halfway mark in the middle of the sail. As the wind drops away lighter, so this crease gets pro- gressively bigger, folding in more cloth so that the shoulders get narrower. The designers of this type of spinnaker say that this is what it is meant to do, that it is supposed to stop it from collapsing, but I do not think it works like this. I have felt for a long time that if you want a smaller spinnaker for light weather then you should buy the correct one and not one with 'cleavage'. They seem to start folding in this crease fairly early on and before the wind becomes very light, and I am sure that a big spinnaker should still be able to stand in these conditions.

The leaches or the edges of the spinnaker should not be too tight otherwise they will curl up to windward in the last two inches. It is equally bad if they are too slack and flog.

Spinnaker boom height

When setting the spinnaker on a run the end of the spinnaker pole should be as high or just slightly higher than the clew. This allows the spinnaker to lift at the head and spread itself, in this way it climbs out a long way ahead of the mainsail and jib into clear undisturbed air. You will find that as the wind drops lighter so the clew of the spinnaker will also drop. To keep the spinnaker pulling at its best the pole should be dropped so that it is in line with the spinnaker clew. Remember to drop the pole so that it comes down horizontally, and not just at the outboard end.

All this also applies when reaching, except that the trim of the sail is far more critical. The spinnaker sheet must be made to move constantly, so that the leading edge of the spinnaker is always on the verge of trying to fold in.

When reaching in light weather the spinnaker pole can be kept much higher than when running because the apparent wind coming from abeam, or slightly forward of abeam, is artificially increased, and this enables the sail to develop more power and to keep itself fuller.

The spinnaker is probably the one sail that you cannot have too many of, as the only tuning that can be done to it is to find the height of the spinnaker pole when it is blowing Force 3 and over. I have found that spinnakers are very critical as to the height of the boom, and it varies too from spinnaker to spinnaker. When I say varies, I mean a difference of only about six inches (15 cm.). On my spinnaker boom I had an internal lift, which came out on the side of the boom making it adjustable. A hook fitted into a series of numbered holes. The variation in the up and down movement, in the end of the boom, was no more than six inches. We used to go out and use a different spinnaker for each race and experiment with the height of the pole over this range. When we found what we considered to be the right height, we marked the clew of the spinnaker accordingly and in following races it was possible to fix the height of the spinnaker pole before going afloat, saving a lot of delay and indecision.

Spinnaker stowing

Always, when stowing the spinnaker away after washing and drying, fold it carefully. If you just stuff it into the bag it becomes a sail with hundreds of small creases in it, and it will be a long time before these will come out to the right shape again. If you have ever rolled a pound note between the palms of your hands as if you were rolling putty, and then opened the note and laid it alongside another uncreased one, you will find the difference in size considerable, the rolled up note will appear to have shrunk. The same thing happens to your sails if they are not properly stowed!

Another warning is to keep cigarettes and matches well away from the spinnakers. This brings to my mind an occasion when I was sailing with David Maw in *Bluejacket* in the Channel Race. We had a run out from the Southsea starting line towards the Forts and we were in the lead. There was a much larger boat just astern of us, coming up fast, with a massive spinnaker. I do not know if he was trying to give us a fright or just trying to be a nuisance. While I was steering he kept coming up dead astern, so that his spinnaker was just over my head. I must admit that I lost my temper and passing the tiller over to another member of the crew I went below for a box of matches from the galley. Back up on deck, with four matches in my hand ready to strike, I yelled at our tormentor: 'If you don't get out of the way I will set light to your spinnaker!' Needless to say we had no more trouble for the rest of the race!

Spinnaker gybing

Just one point before we leave the subject of spinnakers: occasionally when gybing from one reach to another the spinnaker can get blown in between the mast and the forestay, and no amount of pushing with the spinnaker boom will get it out. I have seen this happen over and over again at the wing mark and the amount of time and distance lost is great. To get over this, approach the wing mark with your spinnaker boom well forward (nearly against the forestay) and the sheet trimmed in well, stay in this position until you are ready to gybe. As soon as you bear away pull the boom back aft, and let go of the sheet until the clew of the spinnaker is up against the forestay. Gybe the main boom over, release the spinnaker boom from the spinnaker and attach it to the windward clew. If you do it this way this snag will not crop up again, because you have brought the spinnaker round before you actually gybe to what is eventually to become the leeward side of the boat. Having set the boom on the new gybe the spinnaker will fill immediately.

To re-capitulate!:

1. Sails should be made up from the very best material available which should have a low porosity and a very smooth surface finish. I strongly recommend that the material has a soft finish rather than a hard one. The soft finish sails seem to lack very little in a blow but have a great advantage over the cloth with the hard finish when the wind is light.

2. The batten pockets should have elastic at the inboard end and should be of the slip in, not tie in, type. The full length top batten is the exception as this should always be tied in so that the tension on the batten can be adjusted.

3. All sails should be washed, dried, and folded neatly before stowing away.

4. Always stick to one suit of sails. Learn how to set these sails and do not keep chopping and changing.

5. Remember to trim the jib in light weather, it is often a small sail but it plays a very important part.

6. Set the spinnaker on every possible occasion when you think the wind is right. Respect it but DON'T be afraid of it.

14. Compasses

Uses—position—gimbals

Compasses are becoming increasingly important in racing. Their uses are many and varied, and it is surprising that it is only in the last two years or so that dinghy and keel boat helmsmen have begun to realise their many potentials. To name a few:

Detecting small windshifts which otherwise may often be missed

When sailing hard on the wind the heading of the boat should be noted and checked every ninety seconds. The basic rule is that if the heading alters to leeward more than two degrees—'tack'—should the heading have come up to windward then, of course, you are on a freeing windshift and it would pay to hang on and tack when the next header comes.

Guiding down each leg of the course

To find the bearings of each leg of the course your compass should have a grid. This can be done at very little expense. Most large garages sell rolls of silver Sellotape, the type used for decorating Minis and small sports cars. Buy a roll of this and cut two strips approximately one-eighth of an inch (3 cm.) wide with a razor blade, position them on the compass to cross at forty-five degrees to the fore-and-aft line. One running from the port bow to the starboard quarter, the other from starboard bow to port quarter (see Figure 40). The two forward grid lines are used for going to windward and we will cover this a little later. The two after grid lines are used to guide you down the reaching legs of the course.

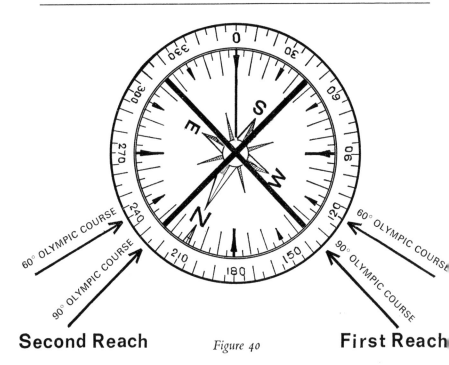

Second Reach   *Figure 40*   **First Reach**

To start with you must know the exact bearing of the windward mark from the leeward mark. This can easily be obtained before the start by pointing the bow of the boat at the windward mark whilst you are in the area of the leeward mark. Once you have this bearing write it down somewhere convenient, such as the deck, with a chinagraph pencil, or better still, buy a few small plastic counters and insert them near the compass for this purpose.

On reaching the windward mark (for example, it is to be rounded to port), bring the bearing of the windward mark (say North) round to the starboard quarter grid line. If the course is laid properly, and you keep North on the starboard quarter grid line, it will take you to within a few feet of the gybe mark. On passing this mark bring North round to the port quarter grid line, this will take you down to the leeward mark. This system works extremely well and is very simple to operate but can, of course, only be used on a triangular or Olympic course. This can be used on a sixty-degree equilateral triangle in which case the lower-ray lines should be changed to sixty degrees to line up with the 60° OLYMPIC COURSE arrows.

Choosing the best tack

The two grid lines on either bow are used for going to windward. As stated before, you first have to know the bearing of the windward mark (say North again). Having recovered from the start and settled down to real tactical thinking, it is possible to look at your compass and see immediately which is the favoured tack. Should you, for example, be on the starboard tack and North comes round past the starboard bow grid line, you will have to tack immediately. On tacking you will find you are nearly laying the windward mark. When rounding the leeward mark and hardening up on the wind, give a quick look to see where the bearing of the windward mark lies in relation to the grid line. It will tell you which tack you should be on. It could well be that during the last two reaches or a run, which ever the case may be, the wind direction has changed slightly. With the help of these grid lines you will easily be able to see which is the best tack to take.

Aids to starting

The bearing of the starting line must be known for each race. The reason for this will become apparent under starting procedure.

Shore bearings

Another use for the compass is to take bearings on the shore, so that you can position yourself on the race course at any given time. This mainly applies to keel boats, but in some cases it can be useful to dinghies, although it cannot be done as efficiently.

Getting to and from the race course

Owing to the increase in demand for races which are held away from the influence of the land and headlands which affect the wind and tides, we are nowadays sailing further and further out to sea. This means that we should know the bearings to get to the course and back again. It may well be foggy, and visibility can easily be so reduced as to make it possible to get lost.

Tuning

A compass can be a very great aid to tuning the boat. Another
chapter deals with tuning as a whole, but I feel that the part played
by the compass must fall into this chapter.

Close-winded ability is the envy of the fleet. The present method of
improving this is by tuning-up races, whereby one can try a different
sail, different mast position, etc., each week, until the magic combination is found. This has been, and still is, a reliable method, but a
quicker one has been devised with the aid of the compass and without
the need for other boats to tune-up against. To do this one must sail
when the wind is reasonably steady in both direction and speed. On
hardening up on one or the other tacks, note the course. You will
find that this varies within five degrees one way or the other, but
you ought to be able to average this out after two or three minutes.
At this time you should be sailing in your normal manner, neither
pinching nor sailing too free. Having decided on the course the boat is
to sail, one should go about and sail as fast and as hard as you can on the
opposite tack, when again the course should be noted. You are trying
to find out the angle your boat is tacking through—it may be seventy
degrees, it may be eighty or even one hundred. It does not really
matter what it is as long as you note it.

Carry out this manœuvre three or four times until you have
averaged out exactly the difference between the two tacks. Having
settled this you can then alter the tune of the boat. It may be necessary
to move the jib fairlead inboard, or move it forward or aft. It may
even pay to pull in the mainsheet, but whatever you do make sure
that only one alteration is made at a time and note each change.
Having done this go over the whole operation again. It may well be
that it makes not the slightest difference, in which case try something
else. Eventually you will start getting a minimum for the angle you
are tacking through. This minimum should be noted, but do remember that tacking angles will alter slightly in different sea conditions
and wind strengths, and this should all be noted in your log. If you
get a new sail, either main or jib, it is possible to check its efficiency
by the above method, remembering that all sails need slightly
different settings.

Using the compass with the wind aft is as important as going to
windward. It has been found that, in the same way that you tack on

windshifts when going to windward, so you should gybe on the
windshifts when sailing downwind, and this can only be done with
the help of a compass. The bearing of the leeward mark from the
windward one is, of course, always the complete opposite to the
bearing of the windward mark which is taken at the start. You must
first decide on which gybe to start the run and this you can work out
at the end of the beat by timing your tacks from the leeward mark,
i.e. the total time spent on port tack and the total time spent on
starboard tack. Whichever is the smallest is the most advantageous
gybe on which to start the run. This system only works if there is not
a strong cross tide, in which case different tactics will have to be used
and these I will discuss later. When running, the maximum speed
through the water is usually obtained with the wind slightly on the
quarter, and if the wind direction is altering all the time this will
mean that the bearing of the boat's head will also be moving. Again,
the grid lines on the compass, the ones you were using to tell the
course on the windward legs, can be brought into play. If, for example,
the boat is pointing the opposite direction to the windward mark,
which is South in our example, and the wind is on the quarter, then
continue on this course, but should the wind alter and come further
aft, then one must luff up to keep maximum speed. Should you have
to luff up so far that due South starts moving over to the leeward grid
line, then gybe immediately and repeat the whole manœuvre again.
This system keeps you more or less on the rhumb-line and travelling
at maximum speed, but please remember again that, if there is a
strong cross-current, one should always try not to get swept too far
downtide.

Types

Because of the part that a compass plays in winning races it is most
important that only the best should be used. It should be easy to read
and dampened to a certain extent, especially for use in the dinghy classes.
It would seem that the ideal situation for the compasses would be to
have one on either sidedeck, just in front of the helmsman, so that he
can keep one eye on the boat and the other on the compass the whole
time. With the problem of salting up of glasses it is also a help to have
them close to the helmsman if his sight is not too good!

In the keel boat classes the compasses should be gimballed, but in the dinghies, where it is essential to keep the boat within five to ten degrees of upright, this is not necessary.

15. *Anchors*

Weight—anchor line—stowage

In most class rules there is a line that says that an anchor of a certain minimum weight shall be carried. I must admit I have always been mystified by this rule. As far as I can remember, since I first started sailing, I have only used an anchor twice, both times in strong tidal conditions when the wind dropped. I suppose the rule is there as a safety precaution, with the reasoning that if a boat capsized and was swept away by the tide an anchor could be put out to hold the boat until rescued. If there was such a tide none of the anchors required by the rules, with the minimum length of line that has to go with them, would ever hold a boat. On the two occasions I used mine I had difficulty in stopping the anchor dragging, even with the very low resistance of an upright boat, and that was also in a flat calm. However, if the rules state that an anchor must be carried, I see no reason why you should not stretch the rule as far as possible to your advantage.

All the anchors of a given weight on the market today are quite good, some better than others in different conditions.

Weight

It goes without saying that the weight of the anchor should be down to the absolute minimum that is required, but one can cheat a little bit here, legally of course, by making an underweight anchor with a hollow stock. If this stock is of a reasonable diameter and has a cap on the end with an eye on it, it can be brought up to weight by using it to stow your tools and odd shackles, bits of wire, etc. The advantage of this can be seen immediately. You do away with the extra weight you would normally have to suffer from the tools that it is always necessary to carry in the boat.

Anchor line

The anchor line itself, as stated before under 'Rigging', can be made up from the rope tails of the main and jib halyards. If this is not long enough it can be supplemented by a short length of line of the same material.

Many boats have their anchor line wound round a drum which looks very nice and tidy, but for the number of times they use it I think it better to do away with this drum and coil the rope up. This can then be tied to the stock of the anchor, so keeping it in one complete unit.

Stowage

Now that you have the best anchor, it is worth while making sure that it is put in a place where it can do the least harm. I would suggest this position is near the centre of gravity of the boat, and as low down as possible. If the boat has a double floor one can always have a small hatch here through which the anchor can be passed and stowed away and the hatch is then screwed down on top. After all, the rule does not state that the anchor must be readily available.

In boats without the double bottom the anchor can be tied or fastened with wire alongside the centreboard case.

If you do ever have to use the anchor make sure you not only let the amount of line you have aboard out but add everything else you can to it. Sufficient line is the only way to stop your anchor dragging. The amount recommended by the rule is usually not enough. The other advantage in having a very long line is that although you are not allowed to throw the anchor ahead of you to gain ground, you can drop it straight over the side and let yourself back on your warp until it is all out. Then by hauling in slowly at first and then faster until you reach the point where the anchor comes away from the bottom, you can probably get the boat speed up to four knots. I am not telling you to sail like this but I have seen it done!

16. Burgee

Types

Now to look at an item of equipment which is very important, but so often overlooked. I was going to call it the 'burgee' but when I looked it up in my ancient dictionary I found that the definition of this word is 'a kind of small coal', so let us call it a wind indicator.

This was originally a rectangular flag of a certain size, balanced on top of a short length of alloy or bamboo rod, fastened to the masthead by a halyard. A number of attempts have been made to produce a reasonably priced, reliable and sensitive indicator. For example,

Plate 36. A wind indicator made entirely of plastic (with the exception of the alloy stem) which is therefore tougher than the average type.

Plate 37. Once round the windward mark the backstay of a Soling must be loosened so that most of the strain is taken by the shrouds. K 30 has not done so and her mast is bending too much.

Peter Cook who is now editor of *Yachts and Yachting*, way back in 1954, made up a very sensitive wind indicator. It was made of balsa wood with frames and ribs rather like the end tip of an aircraft wing. Swivelling on a needle bearing it had a balancing rod stuck out on the opposite side so that, when held horizontally, the vane also remained horizontal. The advantage of this was that it was light and, being of an aerofoil section, it was very sensitive and, because it was not made of flexible material, it was steady and gave a positive reading of the wind direction. Peter Cook made me one of these which I used for about five years and it only needed a new covering in all that time. I am afraid it eventually met with a sticky end when the cat found it in the garage one winter and decided to eat it. I was unable to make another like it myself, not having as much patience as Peter.

Since then we have used solid vanes, but these have not been aerofoil in shape and therefore were not particularly steady, so the flag indicator came back into use once more. The cloth flag however, did become smaller and more efficient, but because of its ability to flap it created wind resistance and it was not until last year that a commercial vane, the Lewmar Windex, came on to the market. This seems to me to be the absolute answer. It does everything that Peter Cook's indicator did but, of course, with modern materials and knowledge,

Figure 41. The 'Windex' indicator which also has guide tabs which can be useful, especially for checking the fastest course under spinnaker.

the needle bearing is considerably more advanced. It also has two wings projecting from it to use as guide lines. It is very light, has very low wind resistance and, of all the indicators I have seen, it is the only one I would recommend. It cannot be used with a halyard, but who wants one anyway. It is supplied with a fitting that screws into the masthead and the indicator stem is screwed into this bracket, so it is removable if you are trailing on the road (Figure 41).

Owing to its lightness it is quite fragile, and great care should be taken when capsizing not to turn the boat completely upside down. If you are in the habit of doing this I should keep a spare indicator!

I did intend writing a chapter on electronic instruments, but as these are being banned gradually by the various classes I am sure by the time this comes into print they will only be used by ocean racers. I must admit I agree, as I consider the great expense of these instruments would be quite restrictive, and in any case I have always preferred trying to sail by the 'seat of my pants'!

17. Stopwatch

Requirements—uses

If you can get over the starting line first it will make it much easier for the race to be under your control. You get a clear wind and as long as you cover reasonably well, it will be very difficult for anyone to get past you. The main snag is, of course, to start first, which is not as easy as it sounds! The greatest asset to this tactical manœuvre is a reliable stopwatch.

As the stopwatch is so important it is not possible to purchase a cheap one which will give you everything you require. The points you should look for are:

1. Guaranteed waterproof.
2. Guaranteed shockproof.
3. Guaranteed accuracy.
4. A large sweep seconds hand and a second smaller minute hand, using the whole face of the watch for either ten or fifteen minutes.
5. On having run the ten or fifteen minutes, whatever it may be, it should be possible to carry on running for a second period of ten or fifteen minutes without having to restart it again.
6. It should be small and compact.
7. It should be very light.

The only one I know to cover all these specifications is made by Huer and this does the job admirably.

Once you have obtained the watch it is then up to you to decide who is going to do the timekeeping, and one thing is certain—it should not be the helmsman! If there is only a crew of two then it is obvious who will get the job. If you happen to sail a Finn then it is just hard luck!

Two years ago I experimented with a small tape recorder, in fact it was so small it used a wire instead of tape. My idea was that one could pre-record the start of a race from the time of the ten-minute gun with a small loudspeaker somewhere under the deck, so that both the crew and the helmsman could hear exactly what was going on. Only just loud enough so that the sound could not reach the other competitors of course!

My recording for the Dutchman went something like this. The recorder was started on the ten-minute gun, the first thing that came out was:

Check all clothing and comfort—nine minutes to go.
Check which end of the line has the advantage—eight minutes to go.

Check cunningham hole tension.

Check outhaul—seven minutes to go.

Re-check course to the first mark—six minutes to go—get near the Committee Boat and stand by for five-minute gun.

Five minutes to go—check rudder and plate for weed.

Check which end of the line has advantage—four minutes to go—bail out all water.

Three minutes to go—start getting into position—if jib is furled unfurl it. Two and a half minutes to go—quick check you are still at the right end of the line.

Two minutes to go—you should be in position for your run in.

One and a half minutes to go—get near the line.

One minute-fifty seconds—forty seconds—get near that line—.

Thirty seconds—twenty seconds—fifteen seconds—start boat moving.

Ten seconds—go like hell—nine—eight—seven—six—five—four three—two—one—GO—make sure mainsheet not in too tight—do not pinch—drive her—keep a clear wind.

The great thing about this tape recorder was that it acted as a check list and saved you having to remember it all as well as reading out the time. It allowed the crew to get on with his job without having to keep looking at his watch, and immediately after the start it reminded the helmsman of the first few jobs he might otherwise have forgotten in the excitement. Like many good ideas this failed on one point, I was unable to get a tape recorder that would time five minutes exactly because the time varied with each recording. I was very disappointed with this and tried various makes, but I am afraid at the moment the small tape recorders are not sophisticated enough to be used for this method. No doubt one day there will be one which is suitable.

In important regattas such as championships, etc., you should always carry a spare stopwatch, purely as a stand-by in case of accident. If you have this second watch tucked away ready in emergency you will still be able to carry on should the worst befall the other. I am astonished at the number of people who have come up to me in a championship start asking how long there is to go because their

Plate 39. Note the differences in mast bend and sail twist on these Contenders taking part in the first official race in Europe.

Plate 38. This rig has all the strain evenly distributed between the backstay, upper shrouds, and lowers. The boat is really moving—look at the quarter wave on the left of the photograph.

watch has stopped. I have always so far told them the right time, but one day I will tell them the wrong time and it will be their own fault.

One thing about buying two watches is that you can certainly ask for quantity discount (I would not mind betting that you get it).

When I mentioned accuracy earlier on, I not only meant this in connection with making sure you start exactly on time, but I was also thinking of timing the starter's gun. At many championships I have been to I have found that the race officer's time-piece is not truly accurate (there was an exception, this was on Lake Geneva in Switzerland!). Usually you find that there is a difference of approximately one to five seconds between the guns in a normal championship race. I do not find this really makes a lot of difference as long as you look for it, because you will find that if the five-minute gun happens to come up one second too early then it is nearly a certainty that the starting gun will come up two seconds too early. If you know this, and can work on it, you can get away a long way ahead of the rest of the fleet. There are times when the race officer may pull the gun one second too early, but this does not usually happen and if you are lucky enough to be at a multiple regatta like Poole Bay Week, where there may well start a class off ahead of you, it is very easy to check the time lapse. If you are the first class off I should seriously consider checking it at the beginning of the week so that you may take advantage of it for the remainder of the race days.

Plate 40. *Shadow* during the 1967 European championships at Bendor which she won, is here seen in winds averaging 35 knots.

Summary: Part 1

I firmly believe a well-thought-out, well-equipped boat can give you a decided psychological advantage over your opponent. If he looks your boat over before the race and decides it is faster than his own he has a definite handicap before the race starts. If you are new to International and Olympic racing you are probably unaware of the 'psychological warfare' that exists on shore between races.

It may be easier to have your boat geared up professionally, but I think it is the personal touch that counts. Your own small designs, adaptations, made with you and your particular boat and crew in mind, could make a difference of a few precious seconds on tacking, etc., that can lose or win a race. Opponents always respect the person who thinks for himself, and can put these ideas to practical use.

Please ensure that your gear is not worn or suspect in any way. Try to keep breakages to a minimum. It is a very feeble cry to come ashore complaining that you lost the race because of a broken item of equipment. This is no excuse at all—the person who won obviously had the foresight to keep his boat in good order and therefore deserves his victory.

At championships there will always be the few who work frantically up until the last minute, tinkering and tuning. I am willing to bet that they will not be among the first six home. The winners will be those who are prepared in good time, afloat with time to spare, and so able to judge the prevailing conditions and feel confident that they are ready in every possible way. Our competitor who launched at the last minute will, in his frantic rush, forget important items such as his stopwatch, be unsure of his compass course, and be wound up to a degree that will effectively stop clear thinking and judgement. If he wins, it will be a fluke!

Determination amounting to fanaticism is a quality to be found in all the top helmsmen and crews. They never stop reviewing their gear, thinking up new ways and methods, not only with the boat but also tactically (both afloat and at the bar)! They are determined to win come hell or high water and the very fact that this determination is so obvious gives them that special advantage over their opponents. So remember—the best boat—the best gear—the best crew—and consider yourself the best . . . and who knows!

Part two:

the crew and the race

18. Prior to an Important Race

Local information charts—accommodation—travelling—insurance—sails—fitness—measurement—food

Preparations for a year's serious racing must be made well in advance. First decide on the number of meetings you would like to attend, arrange it so that you have an ultimate goal—say the World Championships—with all the meetings prior to this date acting as training sessions. Nobody can expect to reach their peak and stay there for an unlimited length of time, so it is very necessary to have this gradual building-up process towards achieving your best when you most need it.

Make travelling arrangements

As soon as you know where you will be going you must set to and make all those tedious travelling arrangements; or better still pass them on to your wife or girl friend to see to!

If you are going across the Channel it is very necessary to book car ferries months in advance, and even then it is not always possible to get the dates you would prefer. Living close to the booking offices in Southampton I have found it easier to go direct to the office, where the staff are very helpful, and it saves time and paperwork in the long run.

If you carry your boat on top of your car it will cut the cost of tickets, if not you must reckon on the trailer costing more than the car rate. The shipping line will need the weight, height, etc., of your *équipage* because they load these ferries very carefully and you could find yourself allocated a place high up on a 'shelf', where your mast would be in danger of catching in the deckhead.

If you carry your boat on top of your car do not forget that winds like the Mistral can play havoc with a high load. I have seen a car towing a high caravan being blown straight across the road into a ditch by one such wind.

We did once toy with the idea of building a collapsible trailer which would go on top of the car for the ferry crossing and which could be reassembled for road trailing at the other end but, unfortunately, this never went further than the paper it was sketched upon.

Just how comprehensive a trailer you will need depends entirely on the distances you envisage travelling. If you are only going to wander around England any ordinary 'backbone' trailer with chocks to support the keel is sufficient but if you intend travelling on the Continent it is another matter. You will be travelling over large areas where, although the roads are very fast, the surfaces leave something to be desired.

Obtain spare trailer wheel and bearings

It is a good idea to carry at least one complete spare wheel and a set of bearings, especially if the trailer you are using is the type with small diameter wheels.

Check with the makers the maximum weight your trailer can carry for any length of time, and very carefully weigh everything when loading the boat to make sure that you do not exceed this maximum weight.

Before leaving home give the hubs a good going over with a grease gun, and then pack the grease gun in the car as the trailer will need regreasing approximately every three to four hundred miles.

If you have to acquire a trailer specially for the trip make sure that it is long enough to suit your boat, and that there is not too much of the boat hanging over the after end of the trailer unsupported. This is vitally important for the longer, lighter boats such as the Five-O-Fives and Flying Dutchmen, etc., which can distort if not supported correctly along the entire keel length. Try and arrange these keel chocks so that each one has approximately the same amount of weight on it and that at no time does any part of the boat rest against the bilge chocks. These should be slackened off so that they are just clear of the hull and will only come in contact if one of the strongbacks or holding down spans break.

The boat should be positioned on the trailer, complete with all the gear inside, so that there is about twenty to thirty-five pounds (9–16 Kg.) pressure on your ball-hitch. You will find that if you make this too light the trailer will sway when it reaches speeds of sixty/seventy miles an hour. Although these speeds are not allowed in England when trailing, it is not particularly fast once you get across the Channel—it seems quite normal to tow a caravan at seventy miles per hour in France! If you do have to stow gear inside the boat make sure that it is padded sufficiently; then if the boat jumps about neither gear nor boat can be damaged. See that lashings are made secure and put padding or packing underneath so that they cannot move. Make sure that all these items are as near as possible to the keel line so that the extra weight will not alter the shape of the boat.

With keel boats travelling by lorry you will have to remember the hazards of tiny villages with hairpin bends, flanked on either side by buildings which almost meet. Although the autoroutes and autobahns are very fast roads, at some stage of the journey you are sure to find yourself travelling on something left over from mediaeval times, and it is well to consider this when packing equipment!

Breakdowns in car or trailer can be a nightmare in a foreign country, much time can be lost, tempers will become frayed and large holes will be made in travel allowances. The answer is to take out Three Star insurance with the AA. This can be worth its weight in gold if you do have trouble. They will guarantee to deal with the breakdown and return your car and trailer home, and fly you and your passengers back to England—a comforting thought when you are towing over hundreds of miles in a strange country.

Boat insurance and other necessary documents

Check that your boat is fully insured in every way for travelling, particularly abroad where you will need extra cover, such as a Green Card for the car, a carnet for the boat and trailer, personal accident insurance, baggage insurance and, most important, medical insurance. Once again the AA are very good at arranging all this for you.

Book accommodation

Apply to the organizing yacht club for addresses of accommodation and book in advance also. Regattas have a way of falling in the middle of the holiday period and traipsing about on arrival, only to find everything already booked, is a miserable and disheartening start to a regatta. In the same way, book up accommodation in advance even if the regatta is in this country.

We have found that the only way to travel around England in comfort in midsummer is to leave home in the early hours of the morning. I hate getting up at three a.m., but even more do I hate sitting for hours in long, dusty lines of traffic. You can always make up those few lost hours of sleep when you arrive at your destination.

When booking your accommodation try and find out where other competitiors intend staying. Anti-social it may seem, but I find it impossible, when racing seriously, to stay with friends who are out to enjoy a holiday rather than race in earnest. Merrymakers raising the roof half the night do not help when you need a good night's rest!

The accommodation need not be extravagant but should be comfortable. On no account skimp on this. It is just as bad camping or sleeping in the back of the car as trying to sleep through a lot of hotel noise. You may think I am biased against camping but, having seen many other sailing friends blown or rained out of camp during a championship, usually in the middle of the night, and having shared a caravan with eight others once, I vote for a decent warm, comfortable hotel with plenty of hot water and interior spring mattresses!

Try and get accommodation within easy reach of the clubhouse. It is a confounded nuisance when things are forgotten or you need different sails if you have to travel miles in dense holiday traffic to go and collect them.

Usually, when representing one's country there is a team manager to make all arrangements for you. This is so with the majority of teams sent by continental countries, but unfortunately only usually applies to Great Britain during the Olympics. Mind you, if your female dependant is well trained and versed in the ways of tetchy helmsmen and crews, she can be like gold dust when it comes to looking after the creature comforts! Very nice it is to arrive in a strange town and be able to get on with the bedding down of your boat while your wife hoofs around the town checking if the hotel is up to standard, finding out the best places to eat and generally getting to know the lie of the land.

Send entry form and copy of certificate

While making all these arrangements see that your paperwork for the regatta is organised also. Enter your boat in plenty of time, giving all the necessary deails. It is a good idea to get a photostat copy of your measurement certificate to send along at the same time, it saves time later.

For the purpose of describing the best way to go about taking part in an important race with the maximum effect, it will be best to go through an itemised account of, say, participation in a World Championship. We will assume for the moment that you have been training hard for the past four months and that you are fit and the boat is going as fast as possible and, most important of all, that you are in the right frame of mind.

Charts and maps

When you have sent off your entry buy a chart of the area you will be racing in, a land map of the hills, and tidal charts showing the strength and direction of the current and times of high and low water and its range, i.e. the difference between the height of high water and the height of low water. Of course, if you have a friend in the Met. Office you may even be able to acquire a set of records for this area (for the dates you are racing) over the last three or four years. Having obtained these aids, and I call them aids because with the help of the information they contain it will be easier for you to make the final decisions when on the race course, you should study them until you know them off by heart.

The chart will show you not only the area you will be racing in, but the depth of water also and this you should note carefully. If you are racing in a tidal area check the depth shown on the chart, as you may well need to put a longer kedge warp aboard. Check also for outlying dangers along the shore, especially when entering and leaving harbour. The last thing you want is to be shipwrecked before ever you reach the starting line!

Occasionally sailing instructions for World Championships are sent out in advance and if this is the case it should be possible for you to plot the course and marks upon the chart. Most good charts give you the land contours around the area as well, but they do not go very far inland and this is where you will need to use the standard map. I expect you are thinking this is a waste of time because you do not intend sailing up the main road, but the idea is to try to determine from this map how the wind will bend across the course.

We all know about windshifts but wind-bends are a little more obscure. The best way to illustrate this is to picture two hills to windward of you with a valley between. You will find that the wind funnels down the valley and then spreads out in the lee of the hills. The annoying thing is that hills up to three or four miles away can drastically affect the wind in the bay in just the same way as headlands do.

Wind always blows much harder off headlands and will always be very fluky under their lee where the turbulence is. When the wind is blowing along the coast, if there is a bay it will swing in and follow the shore round. There are also wind-bends when the wind blows directly on shore, as again it is looking for an easy route. It will not go directly up a mountain if there is a valley next door and in just the same way as it funnels in it will fan out when blowing offshore. We found this in Mexico where, although the wind was blowing onshore, if you moved along the coast a little to where the mountains inland disappeared, the wind altered direction.

Wind-bends have only just started being used in racing, although I understand that the knowledge of this phenomena has been with us for some time! It is possible, by mapping the valleys and the hills, to work out the wind-bends for any direction of wind with an amazing degree of accuracy.

A very good example of wind-bend can be seen at Poole Bay. With the wind anywhere between west and south-west you can start the beat pointing very high on port tack until you start nearing the land, here the clear air comes over the flat land to the right of Purbeck Hills and, as you get into it, it heads you hard. Unlike a windshift you do not tack immediately you reach a wind-bend because it is essential to get right into the new wind before tacking. If you do this you will find you can virtually lay the windward mark on the

other tack. I think everybody feels that with this wind direction at
Poole you should always come into the windward mark on starboard tack.

Tide tables

The times of high and low water will give you the time the tide
will change from one direction to another and, unless there has been a
strong wind blowing for a good length of time in one direction, this
change of tide can be timed accurately. Knowing the heights of high
and low water gives you what is called the range, and if you happen
to have an Admiralty Tidal Chart for that area, you will find a graph
in the back, to work out the strength of the tide at any time in any
given place between high and low water. Write all this information
down to take afloat with you. You know the time of the start and the
amount of time allowed for the race so you should be able to write this
information down for every half-hour. With all this in the boat you
should be able to tell at a glance which way to go up the windward
leg, which side of the rhumb line to keep to when reaching, and so on.
Compile this table for each individual day. If you work out a table
for the whole week in one go and get in a tight corner during the
race where you only have time to rely on your memory you will
find it impossible to single out any one day.

On the road

When packing the boat prior to the journey, remember that
centreboards should be taken out and put in a sailbag stowed in the
car, as there is nothing worse than leaving the centreboard in position
in the case where it can flap and jump up and down and so ruin the
finish.

Sails can travel in the boat, they stow easily and are light. If they
are inside the car they only take up valuable space for heavier gear.
If you can manage it a bottom cover in addition to a top cover should
be used for long distance travelling. It will stop chippings from the
road as well as mud and tar hitting the underside of the boat. If you
do have a bottom cover lash the top cover down firmly over it with
shockcord as it is possible to run through a variety of weather con-

ditions in one day's travel. The cover shrinks from wet to dry and the shockcord can deal with it without worry. The covers also protect the gear in the boat from theft. Once the covers are on lash the masts on top. You will need two if you are going far from home. Halyards on these masts should be tied to the spar with string or Sellotape to stop the continuous rattling which would otherwise take off the surface coating. A sailbag should be put over the base of the mast covering the ends of the halyards, the gooseneck, cunningham hole gear and anything else that may fall off en route. Securely fasten the mast to the after end of the boat and to the mast support at the forward end of the trailer. Always wedge two masts firmly apart with packing material so that they cannot rub together. When this is done fasten each mast individually to the holding-down strap on the boat. It is a good idea to pre-bend these spars in doing this and then you will find that the continuous flexing caused by the uneven road surface is eliminated.

Some time before leaving check that all your lights are working correctly and have the car serviced a good three weeks before leaving in case there are any major jobs to be done.

Check boat measurements before leaving

In International competition your boat will always be measured. If it is a World Championship and you are representing your country then the whole boat, including mast, sails, etc., will go through the mill. To make sure you are perfectly legal carry out your own measurement before leaving. Just pretend you are the measurer— and a meticulous one at that! Try and find ways and means of making the boat illegal, go over everything with a fine-tooth comb. Do not rush it but spend two or three days at it. You need not worry too much about the position of the black bands and the sails at this time.

In *Shadow* we were measured eight times in two years and, although it was the same mast, we actually had to move the black bands after each measurement. I am still at a loss to know why! I suspect each measurer has a tape measure slightly different in length to the others! —or perhaps differences in temperature can cause the difficulty.

Sails were a problem until I found out quite by accident how to get through the measurement control, legally of course. It really is simple.

When you buy a sail it will be as near as the sailmaker can get to the maximum dimensions. If you sail with them they will stretch and therefore will exceed these dimensions. The answer is to shrink them and this is the way I do it.

Three weeks before a regatta I wash the sails thoroughly in fresh water and if possible dry them in the sun, but on no account do I I sail with them or stretch them, I just lay them out flat on the lawn. When dry they are neatly folded without stretching and (without the sailbags) placed in the airing cupboard for two weeks. It means I have to pay for all the family wash to go to the laundry for that two weeks but it is worth it! The sailbags have the same treatment, and on departure sails are put into sailbags, and the whole lot goes into polythene bags, where they stay until the time for measuring. If you do this you will find as I do that the amount of shrinkage is enormous. Once they have been measured you will find it only takes two or three hours sailing to return them to their original size. I learned this trick when I had a spinnaker that was an inch and three-quarters too wide on the half-height measurement. I had measured it myself a week before and found it correct, so was a little worried about cutting it, so to make it legal for the meeting I had a pleat sewn in it. When the series was over I took the pleat out, washed the spinnaker and stowed it away in the airing cupboard. Shortly after we went to another regatta where I presented it for measurement (without pleat) hoping to get away with it! To my astonishment it had shrunk two and a half inches whilst in the cupboard! Since then I have always put all the sails in the airing cupboard before an important meeting, and so far have only failed to pass measurement once. (It is costing me a fortune in laundry bills!)

As International racing calls for travelling long distances it is essential to keep up your standard of fitness on the journey. Other countries realise this need and their teams are flown to the country the regatta is taking place in, whilst the boat is transported by road. The team arrives at its destination fresh and fit for anything. Unfortunately, we in this country do not have the necessary money or backing to enable this to be done, so it is left to the individuals to find their own means of transporting boat, gear, crew, etc., and this usually means trailing the lot across country themselves.

During the three years I sailed in the Flying Dutchman class we travelled a total of thirty-one thousand miles, much of it with the boat. At first we found the many hours cramped up in the car with sailing gear, luggage and wives, an ordeal to say the least. The boredom of many hours continous driving led to indiscriminate munching of biscuits, sandwiches and sweets, etc., ruining the preceding weeks of careful weight watching. By the time we arrived at our destination we were exhausted, bad tempered and overweight. Eventually, we worked out a system whereby each driver did one hundred miles at a stretch then, before changing over, we had ten minutes to stretch our legs.

Arrange the travelling schedule with your crew, allowing time to travel in comfort without any tight time schedules to meet. See that you have food and liquid in the car, but make sure it is of the non-fattening variety and if the drive is a very long one arrange to stop overnight at a small hotel. Continuous driving through the night will mean frayed nerves and worn out crews at the other end. The whole business can be very pleasant if tackled with a little common sense.

On arrival at your destination book in at your hotel, have a bath, a meal and unwind. Do not bother about unpacking the boat at this stage, report to the regatta office, with your original measurement certificate, meet old friends and enjoy yourself until the tension of the long journey has abated.

19. *On Shore*

Tallies—check lists—food, water, comforts—weather reports—gear for the day—check all fittings—read sailing instructions—wash boat

Having arranged your accommodation and had a good night's rest we now have to unpack the boat but, before you start, find out from the regatta office where your berth is.

Obtain the best berth and unpack the boat

At many important meetings the berths are laid out beautifully in rows and numbered so that there is no problem of 'first come first served'. Occasionally they are not in numerical order or allocated and, if this is so, it is essential to try and find yourself the best berth. This need not necessarily be the one nearest the slipway, or to the beach, or the water tap. The trouble with these particular berths is that they are usually right in the main gangway or close by, and the chances of other boats damaging yours are considerable. A good position is in a corner, not right alongside the beach but not too far away, roughly a length of the water hose away from the tap, and a good distance from any overhead high tension cables. Try and choose the hardest piece of ground to put the boat upon, remembering that gravel is fine when it is dry but it can turn into thick mud as soon as it starts to get wet. The best place is on concrete or timber.

Once you have settled the position of your berth start to unpack the boat. This should be done very carefully without spreading your belongings all over the place. When the day ends everybody is rushing around in confusion, putting away all their gear, and although not intentionally, bits and pieces are sometimes tucked away in the wrong boxes. Many a time I have arrived home with a strange pair of pliers, screwdrivers and a few strange socks! I've also lost the equivalent of my own!

Plates 41 and 42. Position at the start is one of the most important parts of racing. F 7 has the pole position but below notice that he has dropped behind H 451 but the boat that was able to free off and gain speed was G 1042 and look where he is now!

Plates 43, 44 and 45. Left. One of the most exciting buoys to round is the Gybemark. In these two Solings you can see that the excitement is just about to begin.

Lower left, the Soling bears off on to a dead run and the fore deck hand, facing forward, is just about to take the pole off the mast. The boat is positioned well and is blanketing the boat ahead.

Lower right, the pole has been connected to the new guy and is about to be clipped to the mast. The spinnaker has not collapsed and this boat has now caught up with the one ahead.

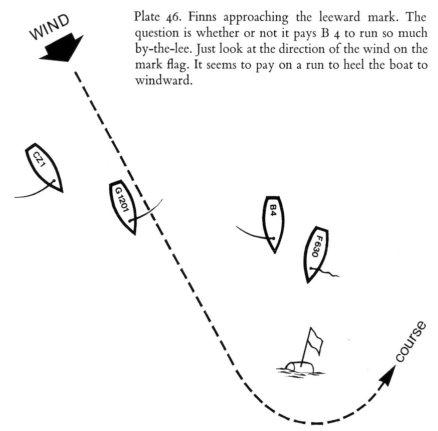

Plate 46. Finns approaching the leeward mark. The question is whether or not it pays B 4 to run so much by-the-lee. Just look at the direction of the wind on the mark flag. It seems to pay on a run to heel the boat to windward.

When the boat is unpacked I suggest you step the mast. Select the one you intend using, and before you actually put it in go over it very carefully. Start from the masthead and work down, checking every fitting to make sure that they are all working correctly and that there is no wear or likelihood of breakages. The clevis pins are always susceptible when travelling and the split pins, or split rings frequently fall out along the wayside.

When you have satisfied yourself that your mast and the rigging is in first class order it is time to fit it to the boat. Please do not forget to check that there are no high tension cables around before you attempt to put the mast upright. If a mast does touch one of those it would melt the aluminium. Sometimes it does not seem to do more than give a hearty kick to the individual holding the mast. Perhaps this is because I have only seen it happen on a dry day, because people have been killed when pushing boats on trailers which have touched such cables.

Once the mast is in try and make sure that all the rigging is fastened in exactly the same way as it was when you were racing at home. It may be a bit late now, but at this point I should like to mention that before unrigging the boat for transporting to this meeting, it would have been a good idea if you had marked the positions of all the shrouds, halyards, backstay (if you have one), etc., so that you may rig it on arrival exactly as it was before.

Check mast tenon is a tight fit

One important point to keep an eye on is where the tenon of the heel plug fits into the hog. As is pointed out in a previous chapter, the mast will not perform as required unless this is very tight. When you were at home the wooden slot that the tenon fitted into was probably wet and swollen and therefore held the tenon tightly, or alternately, the tenon may be corroded or slightly dirty. If you have travelled to a regatta abroad the chances are that the heat has dried out this slot and you find when you catch hold of the mast you can twist it slightly, first one way then the other. This must NOT be allowed to happen, it does not matter how small the movement, it must be corrected. There must be NO movement in this tenon.

The mast gate of a wooden boat is another position to keep an eye on, as it may dry out and get slightly bigger. If this does happen it is quite easy to put in a shim to bring it back to normal.

By the time you have finished with all these items you will be feeling like a meal, so stop work for a while, find a pleasant restaurant nearby and have a decent meal in comfort. On the way back to your boat chat to the other competitors. This is a good time to find out who will be doing the measuring, and what special points he will be looking for. It is important to find out the day for measuring when you arrive, and this is usually two to three days prior to the practice race, depending on your place on the list. It is a wise precaution to go for a sail, with an old suit of sails, before you are measured just as an insurance against the boat having dried out on the journey. It only takes a few hours to replace the moisture you may have lost, and it will remove any worries you may have about being underweight.

When you get back to your boat, go over all the fittings with a fine-tooth comb to make sure that vibration has not loosened anything. At this time it is worth oiling all sheaves, jamb cleats, self bailers and so on, and not forgetting the spinnaker boom end fittings. I try and check here that I have everything that I may need during the coming racing. The only way to do this efficiently is to hoist the sails whilst on the trailer, fit the rudder and generally make the boat ready for sea. Any missing items of equipment will soon be noticed, such as battens, shackles, etc. This way you will have time to find replacements if necessary. When you are satisfied that everything is shipshape, quietly and efficiently pack the boat away without going out for a sail, leave that until tomorrow when you are fully rested.

Learn sailing instructions by heart

The work on the boat being finished, sit down to study the sailing instructions. Generally speaking these are all identical, except for one or two small points, such as the one- or five-minute-rule, the type of signal to be hoisted for it and the limit of the area for the operation of this rule. Read through these instructions very carefully, they must be memorised—word perfect. I find the position of the finishing line is always an important point because, although there is plenty of time to study the starting line while it is being laid, the only time you are able to see the finishing line is halfway up the last beat. It is very difficult then to see at what angle it is laid, and even which buoys are forming it. For this reason pay very special attention to the finishing procedure.

Sometime during the evening go down to the club and join the throng around the bar, keeping your ears open. Some of the competitors will have arrived before you and already had time for practice. These are the boys to listen to and many items of interest may come your way!

If there are any local boatmen at the bar, buy them a drink and start a conversation. Ask their opinion on the weather for the coming week—if it does blow, from what direction it is likely to come; how rough the sea will be and whether there are any violent eddies or unusual obstructions on the course, i.e. nets, lobster pots, etc. If you are racing from a harbour you will want to know the signals that restrict the movement of traffic in and out. Find out from these people the best places to eat and where the local chandlery, banks, etc., are and their times of opening. This information will be useful later on. These boatmen are generally great characters and some of the stories they have to tell, tall or otherwise, are worth listening to.

Do not get carried away and spend too long in the bar, or drink too much. Even if it is only fruit juice, you do not want to be hopping in and out of bed all night! The time to go off to bed is entirely your own concern—some people are lucky enough to need very little sleep, others must have a good eight hours—what is important is to have the amount you personally need to keep fit and to go to bed at the same time each night. Once the regatta is over you can paint the town pink, providing, of course, celebrations are the order of the day!

The following morning try to get up at a reasonable time to allow for a good breakfast and a few minutes run around the block to limber up. Go down to the club if it is close at hand, more boats are bound to have arrived during the night, with the owners still tucked up in bed. As these boats are probably still not unpacked you will have a good opportunity to look at their spreaders, hounds, top of the mast, etc. Once the mast is up it is difficult to see these things— you never know, somebody may have a good idea you would like to copy later.

If you have to pass a paper shop, buy a paper just for the sailing news! Leave world problems to get along without you worrying about them for a week. This all sounds very extreme, but in international sailing one needs to be completely single-minded and unworried in order to achieve the concentration that is necessary. While you are in that paper shop you can stock up with postcards for the week, that is if you bother to send them. I find they are a waste of time when abroad as, nine times out of ten, the cards I send arrive home some days after I return!

Once again have a good breakfast and try to drink a considerable amount of liquid as it is very easy to become dehydrated. This is one of the most unrecognised hazards in competitive sailing. It is not easy for a layman to diagnose but, as far as I know the two main symptoms are extreme lassitude and fewer visits to the heads! This all adds up to errors in judgement. For example, if you were dehydrated, you would find it difficult to bear away, just close enough, to a starboard tack boat without hitting it on the transom. In the Olympics in Acapulco, where the temperatures were very high, many people suffered from these symptoms and, during the period before the start, I saw many a collision. On one of these occasions two helmsmen sat and looked at each other, their boats on a collision course, and neither made any attempt to do anything about it until, crash, they made contact! The bang could be heard halfway across the bay. There, we had an added danger, if dehydration became excessive, the person could go into a coma which, if not observed, within three or four hours could result in death. You are probably thinking that it is unlikely that you will be sailing in conditions as hot as these, but dehydration can occur in much milder climates just as easily, though not of course as severely. How many times have you come ashore after a race and felt you could not get enough to drink to quench your thirst? Have plenty to drink before you go afloat and take plenty of liquid refreshment afloat with you.

Sail out on the course

Now is the time for you to have a practice sail before the measuring day commences. With plenty of food and water aboard sail out to the area to be used for the racing. If it is a fine day take your tidal and land maps with you, as now is the time to find your bearings. Set up the chart where you can see it clearly and as you leave the land pick out the various land marks, and buoys that mark the channel, try and learn the names of the headlands too. Do not bother to sail flat out—this is just a sail to find your way around.

Whilst out there, find a lobster pot or buoy and check the direction of the tide against your tidal chart. If your chart shows it is due to change within the next hour it is worth hanging around this mark to see the exact time of change from one direction to another. Check it against your tidal atlas to make sure it is correct. If you are racing in a bay, try sailing from one end of the bay to the other, check the direction of the wind before you start and again when you reach the other side of the bay, then return once more to your starting point to see if the wind has changed there at all. You will probably find that the wind is completely different at one end from the other; if this is so mark it in on your chart.

Before going back to harbour take a final check on the wind direction, if you checked before leaving harbour that morning you will be able to see if the wind has swung during the two or three hours you were out. If the bay in which you are racing is facing south, or more or less south, and the wind is onshore, the wind usually swings to starboard as much as ten to thirty degrees during the hours between 11.00 and 15.00. If it is going to do this the sooner you know about it the better.

After familiarising yourself with the general area, make tracks for home. Unrig the boat, wash down and stow everything and then anything found amiss during the sail should be corrected. If you are to be measured the following day it is not wise to remove the mast at this point. The safest place for it is upright in the boat. As soon as you take it down and put it alongside there is a danger of people stepping on it and so on, so leave it until the last minute. Get the cover on the boat before it has time to dry out, particularly if the weather is very warm and dry. There is no point in allowing this to happen just before the measuring!

It may seem to be putting too much emphasis on getting the boat past the measurer, but nothing I have suggested is cheating. All you are doing is taking the necessary precautions to stop the boat becoming lighter owing to abnormal conditions which the measurer will certainly not take into account. A few years ago, at the Burton Trophy week in Wales, the weather was very dry and hot; and during

the week it stayed the same. When the dinghies were weighed I
understand that all but one was underweight. One boat had lost as
much as seventeen pounds (8 kg.), and was, of course, ruled out but,
only two months before, this boat had been measured and was two
pounds overweight!

Not only wooden boats have this trouble, fibre glass also suffers
from water absorption. In the World Championships in Montreal
in 1967 Hans Fogh had a Flying Dutchman loaned to him which
was made of fibre glass. At the measurement the boat weighed
in perfectly, but on being re-measured again a few weeks later
it had lost fourteen pounds (6·5 kg.). Therefore, you must be
just as careful weightwise with a fibre glass boat as with a wooden
one.

Analyse your findings for the day

When you return to your hotel settle down quietly to analyse
your findings for the day. Did the tide change at the buoy at the
time given on the tidal chart? If not, did the wind have anything to
do with it? Is your watch accurate? Were there any noticeable wind-
bends over the area in which you are going to sail? Did the wind
gradually follow the sun round during the day; and was the sea
rough for the wind strength? Was the sea coming from the same
direction as the wind?

This is probably a good time to discuss one aspect of going to
windward in a chop. If the wind is blowing hard at the start but
gradually drops throughout the first beat, you will find that the wind
will drop faster than the sea. Always when beating to windward one
finds there is one tack when you are heading straight into the waves
and another when you are going more or less along them. When the
wind is dropping faster than the sea it is vital that you go off on the
tack that drives you straight into the waves. With a dropping wind
one has to get through these waves quickly while the wind still lasts.
If you can put a long tack in while the wind is still there then when
it drops, so much that the waves are killing all your speed, you can go
about and sail along them. If any of the other competitors are foolish
enough to go along them when the wind is blowing hard, when they
get to the end of the tack and try to go through the waves without

sufficient wind to drive them they will go up and down in the same hole. If the wind is on the increase then this manœuvre is reversed.

Get the boat ready for measuring

It does not help to get in a panic about the measuring. When the day comes unrig the boat, not forgetting to put the sailbag over the bottom of the mast to stop the bits falling off. Lay the complete mast with all the sails on top of the boat, so that it is virtually ready for sea, and take it to the measurer like this. When you arrive there you will probably find he has split the measuring area up into several sections; one to measure mast and booms, another the hull, and another the sails. When this happens I use the boat as a base and I personally transport all the items of equipment to the different measurers. As soon as they have finished I take everything back to the boat and in this way there is seldom any loss or damage to gear. I find it advisable not to take part in the measurement procecure, and certainly not to take the other end of the tape! Stand back quietly and watch. See how he goes about it. He may well want to ask you questions regarding the type of material fittings are made of, or how they are fastened, and so on.

When measuring the sails you will undoubtedly have to queue as many skippers present a millionaire's hoard of sails, and there is always a long waiting list for the measurer. Quite often this is a most interesting place because you can have a close look without offending anybody. Of course, it is essential that you should have taken the sails out of their polythene bags before presenting them. When your turn comes keep a close eye on the point they measure to, whether it is the cringle or the outside edge. Although this is laid down by class rules measurers often have their own interpretation! As long as your sail is in—keep mum! Should it be slightly out on any one point do have a quick check to ensure that they are measuring strictly in accordance with the rules. Once the measuring is finished (and I hope yours are all within the rules) return these sails to the boat as they will be needed for the weighing, since the majority of international classes state that there is a minimum all-up sailing weight. This includes practically everything you sail with, paddles, battens, sails, boom, mast, centreboard, rudder, tiller and so on. It is all piled up in the boat with the mast on top. If there is no lifting point a sling is put around your boat and the whole lot is lifted in the air. If you have done your homework properly, and have not allowed the boat to get too dry, she should be no more, no less, than two to three pounds (1 kg.) over. Two or three pounds is as near as you dare take it, owing to the discrepancy in different weighing machines. As this is usually the final measurement taken we hope that, with the exception of the black bands which I explained before are rarely in the correct position, the boat measures. Even if you are very confident, before presenting the boat, that it is legal, it is a terrific relief when it has been confirmed for you by the measurer.

Take the boat back to her berth, and paint on the new black bands on mast and boom. If Sellotape is wound round the mast or boom with one edge in position where the black band should be and a parallel piece placed slightly apart from the first piece, it is a simple matter to paint the gap between the two. Peel off the tape when the paint is dry and you will have a neat unsmudged black band.

Just before stepping the mast ask the measurers to check these bands again. When you rig the boat this time it should be for the week; you should not have to take it down again unless it is for repairs.

Practice out on course

The time has now arrived to bring yourself up to peak performance and this means practice and more practice. Unless the weather is impossible try to get out, for the days remaining before the practice race, seven or eight hours a day. From the moment you step in the boat it must be sailed as if you were seriously racing. I know how difficult this can be when there is nobody else to chase. I am afraid it is just a matter of will-power; tacking, gybing, spinnaker hoisting, spinnaker lowering, all of which can be executed against a stopwatch. If you can find a couple of good transit marks on the shore you can even practise starting. Without other competitors to worry you, you should be able to hit that line on the right second, going as fast as the boat will carry you. If you cannot do so keep on trying until you can. Try sailing the first beat; imagine the whole fleet is in hot pursuit behind you; encourage your crew to drive the boat to the limit. Do not spend too long on any one leg. Practise tacking in the type of sea you will be racing in, as all seas are slightly different it will take you some time to get this knack.

If you can find a mark out on the course round it from every direction, from beating, from reaching and from running. Gybe round a mark from one close reach to another with the spinnaker up without the spinnaker collapsing. You will find it surprising how many times you will have to do this before you can get round properly!

To me the most boring part of training is running before the wind because, without competition, it is very difficult to get up enough enthusiasm to work hard enough on this leg of the course.

By this time there will probably be others out practising too. I am never absolutely sure whether it is a good thing to have a trial run against them at this stage. Generally I think it better to leave them alone, because if they find you are going faster they will retune their boats to reach your speed (and we do not want this, do we?). If you find they are going faster than you, you will lose much of your confidence and if you start to retune you may probably ruin weeks of careful work. Leave this competition until the practice race.

If you can carry out all these manœuvres for three hours during the morning take a rest at midday and come ashore for food. Once your digestion has done its work get out there and go through it all again, even harder than before. Be unmerciful with yourself and your boat because if anything is going to break, now is the best time for it to do so.

After your first day of practice check the boat over carefully to see that nothing has been strained and all is in working order, and if any repairs are necessary see to them immediately.

After dinner that evening settle down and once again analyse the day's sailing. One thing to consider which is often overlooked is whether you could have been more comfortable in different clothing. Wet-suits are a necessity in winter, but as soon as possible revert back to normal clothing. A wet-suit does restrict movement somewhat and can sap energy enormously. A very interesting new suit on the market is called the 'Polar' suit, made by Helly-Hansen. From the outside it looks like an ordinary cotton track suit, but inside there is a surface of three-eighths of an inch nylon fur which, when worn next to the skin creates an insulation layer in a similar way to the wet-suit. Worn under oilskins these are particularly comfortable for keel boat sailing.

If the sun is very bright you might find it helpful to wear a pair of polaroid sun glasses to cut the glare. Be careful that they do not distort distance particularly when you are racing at close quarters.

On a very hot day some people may find it helpful to wear a sun hat—it is essential that the helmsman does not wear one on the windward leg or the reaches as he should be able to feel any variation in the wind strength, on the back of his neck and ears. If you or your crew wear hats of any description make sure they are small and compact to avoid any extra windage!

If the practice race is to be the following day another point to consider is the time it will take you to get the boat prepared and sail out to the course. Allow yourself plenty of time, make sure you are up early enough, work out how long it will take you to get to the boat, prepare and go afloat, etc.

Suppose this is the morning of the practice race; you will not need to do any very energetic exercising as by now you should be at peak performance, and it is just a matter of staying there for the next few days. Arriving at the boat in plenty of time, and with all the gear you will need for the day start your preparations. If tallies must be taken afloat as a safety precaution make sure it is one member of the crew's job to collect this each day. Check the weather forecast yourself, study it carefully and make notes to use later on. The main points being force and direction of wind, and the possibility of fronts coming through later. These forecasts will never be one hundred per cent accurate for the simple reason they are compiled some seven or eight hours in advance. Use them merely as a guide to the sails you will need, the tactics you may use, and the clothes to wear afloat.

Study the weather

If you study weather as a hobby it is possible (depending on how good you are) accurately to forecast the weather to be expected in the coming hour.

David Houghton, the weather expert with the '68 Olympic Team, could tell from his barometer, temperature gauges and balloons which were launched each morning, the weather to expect each day, with incredible accuracy. He did something I have never known before and which was that he predicted the time the wind direction would change to the nearest five minutes, and where this change would occur. As far as I remember he was only wrong about five times in three weeks!

When you have finished studying the forecast decide the clothes you will wear that day; if it is very changeable take out warm clothing in a small sailbag to add extra layers if you need them before the start. Anything you do not need can be handed over to a rescue launch until after the race. Try and keep your clothes dry until the last minute, wet clothes mean added weight and even that infinitesimal amount will slow you down at the start when you need the greatest amount of acceleration.

Food and drink

Check over the food you will be taking afloat. Concentrated rations are available which are ideal for this purpose. They come in three types: food for long periods of energy, food for medium periods of energy and food for a quick burst of energy. Packs of oatmeal bars and cheese and biscuits, come in the first category, raisins, chocolate and fruit (dried), also in highly concentrated form, cover the second, and glucose tablets the third. Just how we use these will be seen a little later on.

There should be an adequate supply of liquid on board, roughly one pint per person per race, unless very hot, then you can step it up to two pints per person. It helps if you add glucose and lemonade powder to the water, it is easier to drink and has that added energy! You should take a drink before you feel thirsty. It is a little difficult, I know, in dinghies especially when out on a trapeze but the answer is to have polythene water bottles with long tube attachments like the racing cyclists use and to suck it up through the tube, rather like a straw. Of course, in keel boats the whole operation is simple.

The check list before sailing (see Appendix)

To return to the boat—this is another time when life is made easier by the help of a check list to run through gear before you go afloat without relying on one's memory which is usually pretty faulty.

Check such things as whether the stopwatch is aboard, spare battens, water, food, sailing instructions, protest flag, and so on. This type of list takes time to make up so prepare it before your regatta. Do not forget to include a complete set of sails to take with you, the weather may change or you could damage the ones you are using. You will need to pass these over with the spare clothing to the rescue launch before the start.

Spare parts and tools should also go out with you such as: shackles, masking tape, seizing wire, pliers and a screwdriver, for example. These major races are generally held some distance from the shore and so, if you break equipment out there, there may not be time to return for repairs.

Now check that all equipment and fittings on the boat are in good order and that they have not been tampered with. It is unlikely that there will be anything wrong with your equipment, but it is essential to do this for your peace of mind! As for the tampering, well, I am sorry to say that these things do happen and it is a point that must be mentioned. Much as I hate it and would like to pretend it does not happen, it does go on at major regattas. You come down to your boat and find a split pin removed, or a screw undone; if you have a dinghy you may even find wet varnish has been applied to the underside of your boat and as you launch wet sand and grit will stick to it un-noticed until you return to shore. Another nasty favourite especially, with one-by-nineteen wire, or even rod rigging, is to kink the wire and bend it straight again. This drastically reduces the strength and it is very difficult to see that it has happened. One way, is to shut your eyes and run your hand quickly over the shroud, if it has been kinked and straightened you will feel a bump in the wire. With the one-by-nineteen construction you are usually safe, unless one strand has actually broken, but with rod rigging where it is just possible to discern stretch marks on the high side, if you look closely, you will have to change the shroud. Of course, other competitors can quite unintentionally alter the adjustments of one or two items of equipment when looking over your boat. A quick check will sort this out.

Before you go afloat wash the underside down either with fresh or salt water to get rid of any grit or salt deposits from the previous day. This will guarantee the bottom is as smooth as it is possible to get it.

Keel boats, that have to be in the water well before the start of the first race, should be rubbed down with a sponge underneath even though the bottom does look clean. Slime and tiny shell fish will slow you down. When boats are in tidal waters it is also a good check to see that no seaweed is attached to the keel or, if it applies, to the spade rudder.

Finally, before leaving the shore check your sailing instructions once again, read through them carefully, make sure you have not missed anything that should be done that morning. It could be that last minute notices have been posted on the club board, a quick look will verify this. If there is anything make a note and take it afloat with you for future reference.

20. Before the Start

Food—check spinnaker is clear—check tacking angle—check if wind and tide are on the move—check bearing of windward mark—check which end of line has the advantage—check for weed—check starter's watch for accuracy

We have now come to the stage where there are certain operations to be carried out, and these operations are the same for the practice race as the others; so what I intend doing is to give you a short breakdown of what should happen from the time you leave the mooring to the time of the start. Later on we will cover in detail the first beat, first reach, second reach, and so on. (See also check list in the Appendix.)

Make boat shipshape

Once your sails are up and you are underway it is essential that the boat is made shipshape, everything coiled neatly and stowed away in its place, the anchor tied down and sailbags stowed—in other words prepare for action!

It is usually a long way to the course and one has time to check a number of points on the way. If it is a run, then use the spinnaker, this will help to get rid of any creases in it therefore making it set better and become a little larger. It will also show immediately if you have your sheets round the wrong side of anything. On no account should the spinnaker be allowed to get wet and so if it should be raining, or there is a big sea running, leave it in the bag until needed. In the Dutchman we used to stow the spinnaker in a polythene bag before we left the shore, we would fasten the neck of this bag with a Japanese slipknot tied in one or other of the sheets (see Figure 42). It was then possible to arrive at the starting line, or even the windward mark, no matter how rough, with a dry spinnaker. Once round the mark a sharp tug on the sheet would release the neck of the bag and then it was just a matter of hoisting away.

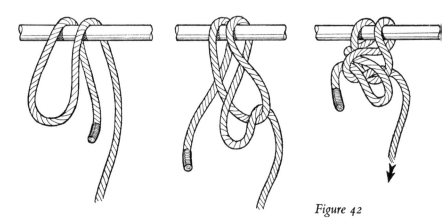

Figure 42

Check for wind-bends

On the run out to the starting line, once well clear of the land and somewhere in the region of where the windward mark should be, check the direction of the wind. Bring the wind directly astern, read your compass course and then check the direction again when you reach the starting area, you may find that it has changed direction. Now this can be due either to a wind-bend or a complete change of direction. Either can be seen quite easily by looking at the boats astern of you, but check if their sails are trimmed as yours were. If they are, it is more likely to be a wind-bend, in which case you can see as you approach the windward mark whether the wind gradually changes to the starboard (or port which ever the case may be), if it does then it is certain that you must approach the mark on this side.

If it is a beat from the land to the racing area then I strongly recommend you check your tacking angle, remembering the chapter on compasses. If you find that you are not tacking through the angle you should, then alter the adjustment of your sails slightly and see whether you can improve upon this. Quite often the waves play an important part in this, but it can usually be overcome by setting your sails to suit waves rather than wind. A bigger sea will generally mean that the sails have to have more power, i.e. a fuller mainsail and a fuller jib. You may also find in this case that the mainsheet traveller can be let out a little, giving you slightly more acceleration. Although you may not be able to point quite as high, it will in the end give you a better performance which will show up as you next tack to see what your angle is.

Check if wind in the gusts is heading or freeing you

If it has been a run out to the starting area this tacking should be done immediately on arrival. Do not just sit around waiting for the start but do a few practice beats to windward to see how you are going and when you are doing this keep an eye open for gusts. See whether the wind veers or backs when the gusts hit you. Mostly I find they veer, but if you can find what they are actually doing it will help later once you settle down for the first beat, because it is quite easy to see these gusts approaching you. In fact on a squally day it is possible to see the gusts three or four hundred yards away, in which case you can tack and put the gusts on the correct bow so that when they strike you are lifted up.

Keep near starting line

If it is a calm day do not get too far away from the vicinity of the starting line and whatever else you do always stay up tide. If the wind does die away one can at least drop back to the line in time for the start.

Half an hour before the ten-minute gun eat your ration of cheese and biscuits or oatmeal pack (tastier than it sounds), and take a good long drink. Immediately your meal is finished check that all your sails and rigging are correctly set up. Outhauls should be checked to make sure they have the right tensions, cunningham holes should be adjusted, and if you are in a dinghy, the centreboard and rudder checked to make sure that there is no weed on them. If there is any water inside the boat it must be removed immediately and a strict eye kept on it to make sure that no more accumulates between now and the time of the start.

Now is the time to pass over the spare sails and the unwanted clothing that you brought out with you. Pass them either to the committee boat or a rescue launch, but make a mental note of where you left them as two or three hours later you will have to collect them!

Tidy the boat up; make sure the food is all put away and water bottles stowed and by this time the committee should have laid the windward mark. Quite often a launch steams off from the committee boat, towing the mark dead into the eye of the wind and this is the time if you can, to get an approximate bearing of where they are taking it. If you are racing in a keel boat the easiest way to do this is by luffing into the wind and holding it there while the crew reads off the bearing on the compass. If it is a dinghy then it is a little more difficult, as the dinghy will not hold her bow into the eye of the wind long enough to take a bearing. The only possible way to do it is by making a sternboard and steering stern first, keeping the bow on the windward mark with the crew reading off the bearing. This bearing should be written down somewhere, preferably with a chinagraph pencil on the deck. By this time the outer distance mark for the starting line will be laid and the committee boat anchored in position.

Plates 47 and 48. It always pays to have the inside berth at the mark. Look at Z 275. He has really forced himself in there but the lower picture shows that he is in a good position for the next leg.

Plates 49, 50 and 51. The first photo shows 99 well in the lead with F 75 just 'exploding' his spinnaker. This is the most efficient way of setting a spinnaker on a Soling. It is folded neatly and held with rubber bands. The crew throws it into the air and all three lines are pulled at the same time. 93 follows round and tailing him is I 75. The next photograph shows I 75 hoisting his spinnaker in the conventional way, i.e. straight out of the basket, and it seems that he then has great difficulty in making the spinnaker fill on this close reach.

Plate 52. Above, on many starting lines there is just not enough room.

Plate 53. Below, who has right of way! 2234's skipper appears to be taking no interest in the imminent collision.

Yachting V

Check direction and strength of tide

Now check the direction and strength of tide and see if it corresponds with your estimates which were drawn up with the help of the tidal charts. In many parts of the world, where the rise and fall of the tide is not very great, there is what I call a surface movement. This is a current of water, not particularly great in depth, perhaps only two to three feet, but always moving in the same direction as the wind. If the wind has been blowing from a certain direction for any length of time then this current will tend to be much stronger and the odd thing about it is, if during the day the wind swings the tide will follow it, but not at the same time as there will always be some delay before the wind can get the water moving in the right direction. The three places I have noticed this happen are the Oslo Fjords, the Mediterranean and Mexico. No doubt there are many other places that it also occurs.

Check wind direction

Having decided on which way the current is running one has then to check the wind direction to see if it has altered since you arrived in the starting area. Remember, you took the bearing of the wind direction when you first arrived and now is the time to see if it has altered. If it has not, well and good, but if it has swung even the slightest, be careful. It could go on swinging that way, or it could suddenly come back. I think if the direction has altered only a few degrees then the chances are that it will come back, but if it has altered as much as ten to twenty degrees it may well settle in this direction or carry on moving round.

In the '67 World Championships in Montreal there was one race when the wind was blowing from the shore, and while we were checking its direction we found that it was swinging backwards and forwards approximately fifteen to twenty degrees, and this occurred amazingly every fifteen minutes. The race officer for the day, quite rightly decided to lay the line at right angles to the average wind, so what it amounted to was that first one end of the line and then the other end paid, depending on which period you were in. We decided to start at the paying end of the line, which was the committee boat end, on starboard, and we got away to a good start. Unfortunately, there were so many boats over the line there was a general recall. Five minutes after the start the wind changed so that the port end of the line paid, and so when the next start occurred fifteen minutes later, the port end of the line had a distinct advantage so everybody started at that end on port tack, and were away to a good start. In the meantime we had discussed the fact that the wind was swinging, and taking a gamble, decided to start at the starboard end of the line to leeward of everybody else—a long way to leeward—again on port tack, which we held for five minutes. At the end of the five minutes the wind started swinging and when it swung through its full twenty degrees we went about on to starboard. We knew that we had approximately fifteen minutes on this tack to get ahead of the rest and as the wind had now put us well to windward of the fleet, theoretically in the lead, we bore off slightly and romped back on to the leaders so that we could get dead ahead of them by the time the next shift came. Of course, this does not always happen, but when it does you should be aware of it.

Check which end of line is best

Now that the starting line is laid, we have the problem of finding out which end has the advantage. I would like to state here and now, before we go any further, that it does not make a hoot of difference which end is nearest the first mark (see Figure 43). The diagram will, I think, prove that as long as the wind is square to the line, whether the mark is nearer one end or the other, you have to sail exactly the same distance from either end of the starting line to get to this mark. The system I use for finding out which end of the line is the best to start on, is very simple, and appears to be accurate. I start by running along the line from the committee boat to the distance mark. I adjust my mainsheet so that the mainsail is just lifting and I lock the main-

Figures 43 (a) and (b). These two sketches are intended to show that if the wind is exactly perpendicular to the starting line, and provided the wind is the same all over the course and the current is the same, then it doesn't matter which end of the line you start from. It is a common fallacy to suppose that the up-tide end of the line is a shorter sailing distance from the windward mark. Of course, if you can lay the windward mark in one tack from either end of the line, then the windward or up-tide end would be the more favourable.

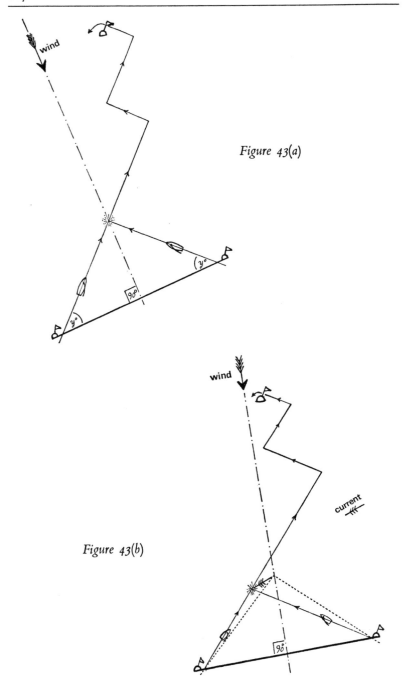

Figure 43(a)

Figure 43(b)

sheet in its jammer and make sure that the traveller is also locked amidships and cannot move, I then sail along the line until I get to the far end. Here I turn around and sail back along the line. It has to be exactly on the line, with the stern pointing to the distance mark, and the bow pointing towards the mark on the committee boat. If, when I am on this tack, the mainsail lifts much more then I know the committee boat end is the end I should start. If, on the other hand, the mainsail is not lifting at all, in fact I can let it out fractionally before it does, then I know that the correct end to start is at the distance mark. Once you get the knack of this it is extremely easy to do it quickly and one does not really have to go the full length of the line. One thing to remember though is not to oversheet your jib as the backwinding of this may affect your mainsail.

Check bearing of line and windward mark

While you are running down the line take a bearing of the actual starting line. First one way then the other. This can be very useful to you later on when you may not be able to get near the line owing to another class starting before you; or if you are round the back of the committee boat on or about the five-minute gun it is possible to do two quick runs on the bearing of the line to check to see if the wind has swung. I did this once at Whitstable and found the wind had swung ten degrees with only two minutes to go to the start, so we went flat out round the wrong side of the committee boat, down to the far end of the line arriving just in time. Meanwhile, all the others who were jockeying for position at the committee boat end had not noticed the wind change and it was possible for us to start on port and cross the fleet.

In most of the important races the committee usually show the bearing of the windward mark as soon as it has been laid. If they do, check it with the bearing you took when the boat towed the windward mark into position. If it is the same, well and good, if it does not agree, which I am afraid does sometimes happen, double check again and make sure that your bearing is the correct one. By this time guns should have started firing, either for you or the class which starts ahead of you. Whichever it is, make sure you get the time accurately. As I said in a previous chapter on stopwatches, very few committees have a clock that runs true for ten minutes. You will find their watch either gains or loses and the practice race is the time to find this out. In my experience I have found that generally the race committees' clocks run fast! In fact, I cannot remember finding one that was slow. From the committee's point of view this is quite good, as the guns usually fire a little early and there is less likelihood that anyone will be over the line. If you know that it is going to fire two seconds earlier you can be just that much ahead, so getting the best position and the best wind.

Ten minutes to go

As soon as the ten-minute gun has been fired check over your boat to make sure that everything is in its place and tuned to the existing weather conditions, and also that there is no weed on rudder or centreboard. This is also the time to suck a few glucose sweets for the instant energy you will need for the start.

21. *At the Start*

Positioning on the line—crossing the line—start of first beat

Your crew should have the stopwatch and should be counting down the minutes. As you approach the time for the five-minute gun to be fired position yourself within thirty feet of the committee boat, preferably on the side from which the gun will be fired. In this way you will get a very accurate recording, since there will be no delay in the time the sound takes to reach you. While doing this keep your weather eye open for other boats because, once that gun has been fired, you immediately come under the racing rules and are therefore liable to be disqualified if a collision occurs and you are in the wrong.

Check for five-minute rule

I mentioned earlier about the one- and five-minute rule. This rule, which restricts anybody from going over the line after a certain time, may be enforced, and this can be any time from the five-minute gun or from one minute before the start. Check carefully with your sailing instructions as usually, if this rule is in operation, there is a signal hoisted to signify it. It sometimes means absolute disqualification if you get into the area between the committee boat and the distance mark and the windward mark; other times it means that to correct yourself you have to cross the line by going round either end of the line which, as you can imagine if it is a long one, can well take so much time that the other competitors will be nearly out of sight! Anyway, one thing is certain—to win a championship one has to finish well in every race—so make a point of being on the line and not over it.

When you have the accurate time of the five-minute gun, go off somewhere where it is not quite so crowded and where you can sail along your bearing of the starting line to see which end has the advantage. Once you have checked this and confirmed that the wind has not changed, start easing back towards that end of the line. If it happens to be the committee boat end, which is usually the starboard end of the line, I would suggest you stay behind it and slightly up to windward, so that you can run down behind it to get into the final position for starting. By this time your crew should be counting down the minutes at every ten seconds, until he gets to one minute to go, then it should be every five seconds—but remember, not too loud— the other competitors must not be able to hear!

Keep near the line

At 'one minute' you should be within a reasonable striking distance of the line and, if in a dinghy, moving slowly, or in a keel boat, moving fast—this is the time to keep cool, do not get in a flap, or worry about getting there too early. Neither should you be worried by the odd boat or two that may come up and thump your transom. You are not interested in them—they should keep out of the way. Do keep an eye on that line, and if you are right under the committee boat and it happens to be a very high one (the race officer will be standing twenty or thirty feet above the water sighting on the line), remember that the first part of your boat he will see is the mast—not the bow, so you can get that much across the line in safety! If you are at the distance mark end of the line then it will be the bow he will see first—so beware!

The start

When the gun goes, if you have made a good start, do not get excited and start jumping around in the boat, sit still and try and bear off a little to accelerate. Most people have a nasty habit of pinching immediately the gun goes, presumably to stop anybody coming up on their weather quarter. This is fatal—you must have speed immediately after the start, and the only way to get it is to free off slightly, which is why you should always try and choose a spot where there is nobody under your lee.

A fault of mine immediately after the start (because I get excited) is that I wind in the mainsheet too hard and too quickly and then wonder why I am not going as fast as the rest. You must always guard against this.

If the recall gun goes, ignore it unless they call your number out, because at this time it would be virtually impossible to get back to the line through the rest of the fleet. If you think it should have been a general recall, because so many people appeared to be over the line to leeward of you—forget it! Race as hard as you can, until you find you are the only one left and that it really was a general recall! I know of many races that have been lost because people who have been in a good position, returned when they thought that there should have been a general recall and when of course, there was not. The people coming up behind, who could hear the guns more clearly, and who knew there was not, have gone on ahead to win.

Positioning yourself for the start is an exceedingly difficult subject to cover as there are so many different conditions to contend with; and also the different types of boats need different treatment as well. I will try and cut it down to a few basics.

First of all, as I have already mentioned, keel boats must hit the starting line travelling at their maximum speed, so they have to have a long run in. Judgement of distances and timing for them is far more critical than on a dinghy, which if it finds it is too early, can backwind the jib and stop with its nose within a few inches of the line, and then when the gun goes, pull in its sails and accelerate quickly. However, it goes without saying that a dinghy that can cross the line travelling at speed will nevertheless have the edge over the others.

I have always found that starting at the port end of the line is very much easier than starting at the starboard end, as you can sail along the line on starboard tack gently reaching and, if you time it correctly, can start increasing speed as the time for the start approaches. This will enable you to cross the line going at your maximum speed and in a reasonable position. If you can be the one to start nearest the distance mark, you will be windward boat when everybody goes on to port tack.

When starting in this manner one has to be careful, if the tide is flowing against you, not to get too far down to leeward so that when you do finally wind up during the last minute, you are unable to weather the distance mark, as the gun goes. It so often happens that the furthest boat along the line leaves it too late, and ends up by having to pass to leeward of this mark, and then has to gybe round and start again behind all the others.

Then, of course, the opposite occurs if the tide is sweeping you over the starting line. In this case one wants to start a little to leeward of the line and one can afford to go even nearer to the distance mark, because if you do happen to get too near it all you need do is 'pinch' and the tide will sweep you round. The only difficulty in these conditions is that you usually get a bulge in the middle of the line owing to the people running down and being swept over, and nine times out of ten there is a general recall.

Starting in the middle of the line, as far as I am concerned, is out unless it is a fixed line with transit posts at the end. I do not believe that anybody can make a good start in the centre of an open sea start line as there is no way of deciding exactly where the line is. I know that some helmsmen say that you can get a transit of the committee boat with the shore, but what happens if the tide suddenly changes or the wind drops or increases—the committee boat moves and this transit goes wild. The only place to start is at either one end of the line or the other where you can be sure of the exact position of the line.

Starting at the starboard end of the line on starboard tack can sometimes be easiest because, no matter what people say, there is always a hole there and it is up to you to fill it! On your approach to this end of the line keep up close to the committee boat so that nobody can come inside you. This, if possible, should be done a little while before the starting gun is due but the exact timing is difficult to state because it depends on how long the committee boat is. In Norway, where they used minesweepers, we had to be off the stern of these committee boats with one minute to go, because the line was taken from the flagstaff situated on the bow; but another type of committee boat could be just a little twenty-five to thirty-foot fishing boat. Once in this position make absolutely certain that nobody comes between you and the boat. If anybody looks as if they intend doing this just give them a 'pleasant' warning smile that there is no room! Oddly enough, you will find that fifty per cent of the people who intend starting at this end of the line will arrive there too early anyway and will start reaching down, so you can forget about them. The rest will be rapidly approaching your stern at this time and it is up to you to make sure that they do not get to windward of you so that you force them right round to leeward. As soon as they start getting to leeward then of course you can blanket them and so start slowing them down. When you have approximately ten seconds to go to the start, get the boat moving. This is where the dinghy has an advantage over the keel boat which cannot do this. Anyway, get it moving and do your best to hit that line on the gun, going fast.

If you have carried out this manœuvre correctly you should find that you are windward boat; nobody will be astern and up to windward, and there will be a slight gap between you and the leeward boat which allows you to bear off slightly and gain speed.

This routine is moderately easy to perform, but changes slightly if the tide is running with you and forcing you over the line. In which case, I suggest that you make a point of arriving at the starting line two or three seconds late but travelling fast. The reason being that seventy-five per cent of the boats starting at this end of the line will arrive very early indeed and there will be an absolute shambles as they all try and bear off along the line. Secondly, because of this shambles, the wind will be greatly cut up in this area. Therefore you should arrive on the line, in the right position, going flat out and able to tack whenever you wish, two or three seconds late. There may well be somebody slightly ahead but I bet my bottom dollar they are well to leeward!

We may well carry out this same procedure with the tidal stream running along the line towards the committee boat. Exactly the same procedure should be followed with the exception, that in a dinghy one can lift the plate right up, or nearly so, to counteract the pull of the current. Do make sure though, that your crew has one hand on the plate ready to bang it down at a moment's notice if you have to carry out some violent manœuvre. Quite often this is one occasion when one does not want to start right under the committee boat but perhaps twenty or thirty feet away, as all the other boats with their plates right down will be pushed hard along the line causing bunching at that end. Anyway, these are only suggestions since one cannot cover every eventuality.

Whilst cruising with my family this year I have had a chance to watch many starts and I have seen many mistakes which I think should be noted. One fault is that many people get too far away from the line in the last two minutes. Secondly, in ninety per cent of the dinghy starts I watched, very few boats have ever been within ten to fifteen feet of the line when the gun goes. In contrast I must say that this does not apply to keel boats which sometimes make a pleasant sight when they start all dead in line. A nasty habit I have particularly noticed in Dragons is that they do not hoist their jibs until some time after the five-minute gun has been fired. This I consider a mistake, as it could well be that there is a snarl-up aloft so that the jib takes longer to hoist, in which case, you will have to go up and free it. The jib is very necessary for acceleration purposes, after all, if you do not want it you can always let it flap. If you need to get out of somebody's back-wind or even out of their way, you can quickly sheet the jib in hard. Lastly, so many choose the wrong end of the line. If the line has been set square to the wind, why not start at the unpopular end—

after all, the distance sailed to the windward mark must be the same, so the person who can guarantee the clearest wind for the longest time will have a distinct advantage.

If when you have started you find somebody is just down to leeward of you tending to slow you up—tack immediately, and clear your wind. If you hang on in this position you will just slow down and lose touch with the leaders. If, by any chance, you have not managed to organise for yourself the 'pole' starting position, all is not lost as long as you make every conceivable effort to stay in the clearest air, even if it means going behind two or three boats to clear your wind and also clear the turbulent water which is knocked up by the quarter waves.

22. The Windward Leg

Tactics—windward mark—sail trimming—tacking—balance—trim—wind-shifts

Tactics on the first windward leg are probably the most difficult to decide upon. Do you go up the middle of the course, or do you keep to port or starboard? There is a correct way, and by the time you get to the windward mark you should know which way this was and be able to use it more or less on the second beat. The point is you must work out for yourself which is the quickest way and get to that windward mark before anyone else. This is where you must take into account tidal information, weather forecast, and wind-bends. These three things combined with the weather conditions prevailing at that moment must be analysed by you quickly and then put into practice.

Using the current

Let us go through the list of items you should consider, and why. First and foremost—the current running against you. If this is the case then it is worth making the first tack towards the shore, where the tide is bound to be weaker. You may even find it profitable to tack up the shore in the slack water until you can lay the mark easily and then tack out to it. Under these conditions you must make sure that you are not forced by other competitors to tack out too early. It is often a good thing to overstand this mark so that you can reach down with the current instead of understanding it and having to tack the last few feet against the current.

If the current is running with you then you must do the reverse and tack out into the stronger tide, being careful not to overstand. If the current is running strongly under you, and you tack when you think you can just lay the mark, you will find you are coming into the mark on a reach as the current will have swept you well to windward; so always make a point of tacking much earlier than you should and doing the complete opposite to what you would normally do if the current were against you.

Using wind-bends

If it is impossible to get out of the current no matter where you go, then forget about it until you are in the vicinity of the windward mark. In this case your only decision will be which is the fastest course with the wind available to you. The snag with this is that, unlike the current which you can definitely say is running at one knot out in the middle and only half a knot inshore, wind strength and direction vary continuously. There is no way of knowing whether the direction has changed, you will only have your own inspired guesses to rely on. If it is a sea breeze then the wind is probably stronger inshore than offshore. If it is an offshore wind then the reverse usually happens. Changes in wind direction can sometimes be forecast but cannot be guaranteed. Wind-bends can.

I would first plan my course to take as much advantage of these wind-bends as possible. Secondly, I would take into consideration the strength of wind and, as stated before, if the wind is dropping I would make my first tack straight into the sea. If the wind was increasing then the first tack would be across the waves. If I had none of these choices then I think that I would choose to keep to the starboard side of the rhumb line because, generally speaking in the northern hemisphere the wind rotates clockwise during the day, and by keeping to this side if the wind does change in the slightest in this direction, one will get lifted up nicely towards the windward mark.

The strategy of covering

I consider that tacking up the middle is a mistake. Usually the majority of other competitors are in this area and we are back again to cut up wind and water. I am sure that one should choose either one side or the other of the rhumb line. It is, however, equally important to make sure that you do not leave the main body of the fleet, after all it is the championship you want to win, not just the one race.

Taking flyers, that is going off by yourself to the extreme edge of the course and coming back, is no good at all to anyone. The chances are that either you will be a long way ahead or a very long way back in the fleet. I must say that I think, generally speaking, it is advisable in a series of races to play safe. Stay in touch with the rest of the fleet and if you see any of them have an advantage over you, it is easy to get back amongst them again.

Another point to remember is that occasionally you may well get ahead, but to one side, of the fleet. If this happens, tack and cross the fleet at the first opportunity. The chances are that a few minutes later you will not be able to do this. It has happened so many times to me and I get so furious when it does, but it is a hard move to force yourself to make—so the rule is to consolidate your position whenever possible.

In one race in a regatta in San Remo I started to leeward of the main part of the fleet and a little further inshore, with the current against me and a sea breeze. This enabled me to romp ahead and approximately three or four minutes after the start I was well in the lead but a fair way to leeward. Looking back, I know I should have tacked then and there to get dead ahead of the fleet to enable me to cover them—instead I carried on hoping to increase my lead. At the time I felt sure I was doing the right thing, but not for long. A few minutes later the sea breeze swung round and free'd the boats behind and to weather of me so that they were able to lay the windward mark without tacking. I swore then and there that I would never let it happen to me again, that I would always tack when I could to cross the fleet, but needless to say it has happened again, and each time I could kick myself!

Windshifts, whatever the type of day, are always there, and should be made use of. In medium winds strengths, windshifts of only three to four degrees should be tacked on, but in stronger winds, when tacking is more difficult owing to large waves stopping the forward motion of the boat as it comes head to wind, then I would suggest that the wind change must be at least ten degrees.

This is also true of windshifts in very light weather where maintaining boat speed is absolutely essential, tacking should be restricted to very good windshifts.

One thing you need not worry about during the first seventy-five per cent of the first windward leg is covering. Everybody will be trying to find the fastest way to the windward mark irrespective of others. It is only on approaching the mark that you should start to worry about those nearest to you. Usually at this time they are all coming back to the rhumb line, so if you are in the lead at this point, and everybody is converging on the mark, try and position yourself as effectively as possible so that you can take advantage of any windshift that may occur in the last minute or two of the beat. It is from this position onwards that you will need to use covering tactics.

Sailing techniques in waves

Occasionally, when racing on the open sea with only a very light wind blowing, there is a ground swell running. This swell may have been caused by a strong wind previously, or by a strong wind approaching. When this is present you need a definite technique to carry you through it. Most of my racing has been done on open water and gradually, almost without realising it, I have developed a technique for this which almost always gets me into trouble with competitors from other countries!

As these swells approach the boat heels to leeward and as the swell passes under you the boat heels to windward. My technique is to reverse the procedure and as the wave approaches and the boat tries to heel I sit out hard, keeping her dead upright. As the wave passes I climb in, sometimes even getting down to leeward. Remember that this is in a wind force of one or two and not a sitting-out breeze. To do this efficiently, keeping the mast upright and still although the boat is trying to move about all over the place, requires a great deal of effort and teamwork on the part of the crew as, during the whole of the windward leg, there is no time when the crew can sit still for even a short while. I remember at Torquay during the Merlin Rocket championship, Tony Fox, who was crewing for me, lost six pounds in one race and David Hunt, when we were racing in the European Championships for Flying Dutchmen at Bendor, lost four pounds. I make no bones about it, it is very hard work but very rewarding.

There is also a secondary feature that comes about from this technique—as the wave approaches you and you start sitting out hard, there appears to be a slight increase in wind strength. I am not sure why this is, it may be the movement of the water or it may be because you are coming up to the top of the wave and are in clearer air and hence a stronger wind anyway. The increase in wind strength allows you to point a lot higher in those few seconds as the wave approaches and is lifting you to the top but, having reached the top, you then have to bear away again until you have dropped into the trough. You then luff up again as you go up the next wave, at the same time keeping the boat dead upright. On account of the part you play in keeping the boat vertical you will go much faster through the water than your competitors and, because you can point up every time a wave approaches, you will gradually creep out to windward.

David Hunt and I used to call this 'pulsing'. In Bendor, where we had very light weather after an extremely strong Mistral, there was a big sea running and we were protested for doing this by one of the organising committee. He had been taking photographs of us. Mind you, we knew all about these photographs as we had seen them trailing us in a motor boat for hours on end! Goodness knows how many miles of film they shot! We were not aware of this protest meeting until nine o'clock that evening when we were having dinner.

Alain Draeger came through the restaurant looking very worried, to tell us that there was this protest meeting against us. Dinner stopped then and there, and off we went to the committee rooms where they were waiting for us. We went in and the committee explained that this protest had been brought against us because it was felt that we were 'rocking the boat' and thereby infringing Rule 60. This rule states: 'A yacht shall be propelled only by the natural action of the wind on the sails, spars and hull, and water on the hull, and shall not pump, ooch, or rock, as described in Appendix 2, nor check way by abnormal means, except for the purpose of Rule 58, . . .' When we asked how they considered we were 'rocking the boat' they stated that we were throwing our weight backwards and forwards in the boat, which in any other type of conditions would have, of course, been rocking. We told them that all we were trying to do was to hold the boat dead upright—which took some considerable effort— and we could not always guarantee that the mast did not sway from time to time, as it would do in any normal boat. The argument went on until very late in the evening and eventually we were asked to leave while they made their decision. We sat glumly outside, thinking that if they did disqualify us the chances of winning the Championships rested on the following day's race, but if they considered we were not infringing any rule then it was already ours, we could not be beaten. We were recalled into the hall and were more than relieved to hear that they were not disqualifying us as in their opinion no rule had been broken.

Eddie Stutterheim, who was on the protest committee, said he was going to take the film and present it before the I.Y.R.U. at its meeting the following November. Whether he actually did I do not know, but I received a letter from him some time later saying that he had discussed the problem with various people and they all came to the same conclusion—that it was illegal and that I should not do this again in a race.

The following year when we were in Montreal for the World Championship, it was again very calm weather and there was no swell around at the time so we did not need to be quite so energetic in trimming the boat. We did find, however, that by 'winding up' into the wind and then bearing away we were able to go much higher than the majority. I think this was entirely due to the fact that there

was absolutely no sort of wave there at all, which just shows how calm
it was! However, Eddie Stutterheim was watching and came up to
me after the race and told me that I ought not to have done it. John
Sully, the South African champion, was nearby and pointed out that
this was something he had been doing for the whole of his sailing
career. Anyway, the arguments are still raging but more and more
people are sailing this way, particularly in keel boats where I think it
pays off even more than in dinghies.

The windward mark

Many races are won or lost at the windward mark and this depends
entirely on how you round it and what else you do in the first
hundred yards after the mark. You must round it with the utmost
speed, do not come in on port and then tack right on the mark. It is
much better to come in a little earlier on port tack and then go about
on starboard tack to approach with plenty of way on. This will also
enable you to get the spinnaker organised before you actually reach
the mark and you will then be able to have it up very quickly immediately on rounding, if you need it (see Figure 44).

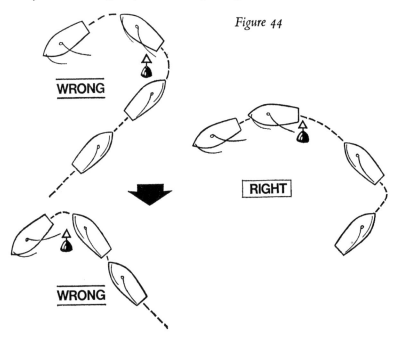

Figure 44

WRONG

RIGHT

WRONG

If you happen to be back in the 'bunch' try and come into the mark on starboard and keep a clear wind, even if it means slightly overstanding it. Come round in a slow sweep, instead of making a violent turn, adjusting the sails as you go.

If you reach this mark in the lead, round it carefully and if you have a spinnaker have it ready for hoisting. On no account hoist it unless you are at least five or six boat lengths in the lead and you are absolutely certain that the spinnaker will pull efficiently. Setting a spinnaker on the first reach is rather like covering on the beats, you should not set it until the second boat has set one unless, of course, it is obvious that it will pay. If you hoist it and perhaps it will not set because the wind is a little too far ahead, the boat behind has only to luff up a few degrees to catch right up to you or even go past. If you wait for his spinnaker to be hoisted, or at least the point where it is impossible for him to luff, it is then safe to set yours. If you are rounding the mark just behind the leader wait until you see his spinnaker going up and then luff! Most of the time the leader will try and cover you, and immediately he does this all is lost, because his spinnaker will not fill and he slows down. As soon as you are level and up to windward you can set yours and be away.

If you are well behind at the first mark, try and take the fastest course to the wing mark. Do not try fighting with anybody—do not luff anybody and if there are boats slightly to windward of you going faster, just let them go. Try and do your best to keep in touch with the leaders, after all they are the ones you want to beat. You will usually find that those who are going faster, and are to windward, will have to run in at the last minute to the mark and then you will be ahead of them again. If you do go out there with them, all those to leeward will pass you, but if you try and stay on a direct line between one mark and the other, you will find the leaders gain practically nothing on you, although they should because they are in a clear wind and you are not. One good tip when you are going down a reach and sitting up on the windward deck, always try and keep the mark you are aiming for slightly on the windward bow. This will enable you to sail a more direct course between the two marks.

Though most championship courses are run port way round there is some talk at the moment of using starboard hand courses during championship weeks sometimes, and this is a point we must cover. In my opinion it is a crazy idea as it virtually stops anybody getting round the first mark if they are all in close company. I hate to think what would happen halfway down a Finn fleet! We must, however, consider what you would do if you were fighting another competitor whilst approaching the windward mark on starboard, and a boat is coming across on port tack. You cannot tack immediately ahead of him and if you go on and then tack he will go under your stern and get round the mark first. If you tack under his lee bow the chances are that he will carry on and, immediately you have to bear away after the mark, he will take your wind and pass you. Under these conditions I would recommend that as you approach the mark and your opponent you slow your boat down so that you arrive at the mark at the same time as he does. If he does not tack then you should be able to cut him in half! If he does decide to bear away under your stern he will not get round the mark, so the only possible solution is for him to tack. In this way you will round this mark with your wind well clear.

If you are coming up to this mark in a long line of starboard tack boats with only half a boat's length between each boat, no one will be able to tack, since they would each be tacking in the next boat's water, especially if the tide was sweeping you all away from the windward mark. It will be impossible to get round because you will just have to go out with the leading starboard boat until there comes a gap astern and you are clear to tack. This is the type of thing I do not like about going around the course to starboard because it almost means that the first shall become the last, which is very wrong.

There is only one way out of this dilemma—when the first boat approaches the windward mark and he finds that he cannot tack because the boat astern is too close, he should start to pinch, and the second boat will be forced to leeward of him. If he has been slowed down enough, then he in his turn will force the next boat astern of him to leeward and there will then be room to tack. It must be done very quickly because the fourth boat coming up behind could romp in and hit his stern before he has cleared the mark. With all this in mind I would like to issue a very strong plea for a 'port about' course whenever there is a large entry of boats.

23. Reaching & covering

Leeward or windward?—spinnaker and two-sail reaching—balance—trim—surfing—planing—gybe mark—the lee mark—the second windward leg

Now we are on the first reaching leg. Once round the windward mark the first thing to do is to check your direction to make sure it corresponds with the compass course between the two marks. When it does, make sure that the sails are trimmed correctly to give you neutral helm. Now is the time to let go the cunningham hole tackle and ease out on the foot of the mainsail. Any tension you may have on the cunningham hole on the jib luff should also be let off and if you are in a keel boat ease off the backstay and try to tighten the forestay, so pulling your mast forward and reducing any weather helm.

In a dinghy it will be necessary to adjust the centreboard and this is extremely critical and depends largely on the sea conditions at the time. If it is very rough I suggest you pull a little more up into the case than is normal, this will allow the boat to side-slip down the big waves which will help you to point a fraction higher than you would normally and so go faster.

It may be that you are in a boat that does not use a spinnaker or the course may be too close for spinnaker work, in which case it will be a 'two-sail reach', but, either way, one has to keep the boat dead upright which means very energetic movements by the crew. In just the same way that I mentioned when going to windward in light airs, in a swell when there is a fair amount of sea and wind one can use this technique when reaching. It is quite incredible how much faster you will go if you 'work the boat'.

One thing you must never do is to sit still, I have seen so many people who, when they have rounded the windward mark, sit back for a rest for the next two legs of the course. These are usually the slower boats—the fast boats being the ones with the crew working the whole time.

Remember, if the wind increases or when you surf down a wave, the apparent wind will come forward so the main and jib should be trimmed in together and, when the wind drops or when the wave has past, then the sheets should be eased again. Continuously adjust your sheets on the reach and never cleat them.

After a long windward leg there may be time to have something to eat and drink. Try to do this at a convenient moment when there is a lull in the wind or you are well clear of everybody, because your sailing will suffer and so will your concentration for the few moments you are tucking in. On the other hand the benefit you will get from this later on will be worth some lack of concentration here.

If, with the new 'sixty degree' Olympic course, you find the first reach is too close to set a spinnaker, then it could be profitable to luff up to windward and set the spinnaker about halfway along the leg. This really depends on the class of boat you are sailing, but it is a possibility worth considering. On the other hand, you could set the spinnaker immediately at the windward mark and sail slightly down below the wing mark, then lower the spinnaker and luff up at the last minute. The disadvantage of this is that you have to hoist your spinnaker twice instead of once if you do it the other way, as the luffing up to windward and then setting it allows you to carry it right around the wing mark and on to the next leg.

Another point to be taken into consideration is the direction of the tide. It may be running across this leg of the course, in which case take a bearing on the next mark and check that it is constant or, if there is land behind it, try and get a transit. The main thing is to sail the shortest possible distance and the only way to do this is by going in a straight line. Do not worry too much about those luffing out to windward of you. I know they go much faster when they do that and come up roughly abeam, but by that time they are a long way to windward and still have to get back to your course. When they try to do this they slow down. What is worrying is when somebody goes down to leeward and comes up abeam. This is dangerous since, when they approach the mark at the far end, they can luff up and come in ahead of you. On the other hand, I do not think this is worth worrying about on the first reach because for you to go down there would probably slow you down even more. The main thing is to try harder and be determined that he will not get round the next mark ahead of you.

Fore-and-aft trim on this leg must be treated with the same importance as athwartships trim. That is, as the wave comes up so that you start surfing, slide forward along the boat and try to keep the bow pointing down. As long as the bow is down and is not slipping into the next wave, one goes much faster. As the wave comes after you and eventually goes ahead of you, come aft to keep the bow out of the water. Once the boat is on a wave it is up to the helmsman to try and stay on that wave as long as possible. If the leg is a very close one, then he will have to bear away to stay on it and if he does this he can luff up later on. If you are on a broad reach and have to luff up along the wave to stay on it, then sail trim is of the utmost importance because the apparent wind shifts surprisingly far ahead.

If you are in a dinghy and you are planing the boat must be held upright at all costs and the bow must be kept out of the water. Do not forget to have the self bailers down (as long as they are of the Elvström type), even if there is no water in the boat as this allows a stream of bubbles to go over the hull and increases your speed.

I should at this point mention centre mainsheets. I have tried various methods of adjusting this type of mainsheet in a dinghy when planing and I have found the best method is to cleat the mainsheet traveller and play the mainsheet itself through a Novex block which is situated in the bottom of the boat. It is hard work but efficient. I still cannot find out why there is so much more advantage in this method, rather than in cleating the mainsheet and playing the traveller. I think it may be because when you adjust the mainsheet it alters the twist in the sail and therefore helps you to keep the boat upright. If you adjust the traveller the twist in the mainsail stays exactly the same, and the amount you have to let out the boom has to be increased. Therefore, it is a much more critical adjustment and so when it is blowing hard and there are steep waves about, you just cannot be quick enough.

Preparation for the gybe

On approaching the gybe mark it is essential to position yourself correctly in relation to your other competitors, especially the ones ahead. As mentioned in practically every other book on sailing: always

Figure 45

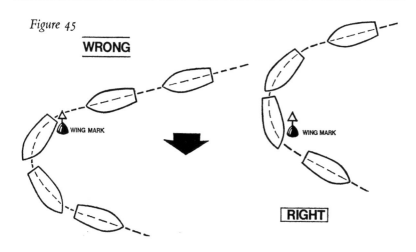

try and come into this mark at a gentle angle. Do not make a sudden turn around it unless you are forced to. If you are well back in the fleet, then I think you should forget this rule and try for the inside berth. If you get this berth everybody else will have to keep clear of you and you will be able to take as much time as you like going round the mark. If you are in the first six and you want to get round with as much speed and efficiency as possible and the spinnaker is up, this is not so easy. You will find that usually other competitors gybe round the mark and end up with half the spinnaker to windward of the jib, and half to leeward. They will disappear rapidly to leeward and so leave a large expanse of water between themselves and the gybe mark! This is where all the hard practice you put in after the measuring will pay off, because you will go round the mark close in, gybe with your spinnaker to leeward of the jib, and promptly go off, well to windward of all the others.

This you do in the following way: approach the mark so that you come down more or less on a dead run. As the need arises—when you gybe pull the guy right aft so that the clew of the spinnaker will be level with the forestay. Cleat the old sheet, gybe hard and keep close to the mark. It will then be possible to trim the jib and main so that you can carry on to the next mark. Your crew now removes the spinnaker pole, if he has not already done so, and fixes it on to the new side. The secret of the whole manœuvre is that the spinnaker must be taken to what will be the leeward side of the

Figure 46

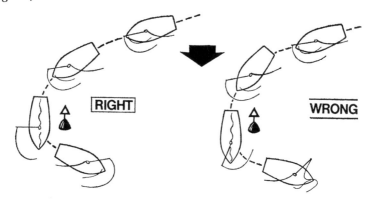

jib before gybing, because if there is any part of it to windward it will fill as a bubble between the mast and the forestay and will immediately kill your speed.

Do not at this point try to get up too high; it is possible that the wind is now a lot freer, so all those people down to leeward of you who made bad gybes will start luffing up to try and stop you coming past. One should get as near to them as possible to get the maximum blanketing effect, but be careful they do not luff you hard. This is unlikely if they have spinnakers up. Occasionally, as soon as you do blanket such a boat, the spinnaker collapses and, if the crew is trapezing, the boat comes over to windward and the mast may touch yours. If this happens you will be out—so beware!

The only other time I think it is necessary to get to windward is if the tide is sweeping you to leeward or if there happens to be a line squall coming up. If this is so you will need to climb as high as you can, so that when the wind does increase you can bear off and run with it, still keeping your spinnaker full while all the others will be hard pressed. They may even be forced to take their spinnakers down! However, the tactics on this leg should be almost the same as the previous one.

Rounding the leeward mark

On approaching the leeward mark try and get another chance to eat and drink and then start adjusting your sails for the windward leg. It is much easier to do at this time than when you are round the mark. If possible, and if the others will allow you to, try and get slightly to leeward of the leeward mark before hardening up so that you can cut that mark as closely as you dare. This will probably mean taking the spinnaker down a little earlier than you would normally do, but I think it preferable, since nothing loses you more time than a spinnaker that is not stowed properly. By the time you have stowed your spinnaker and if you are far enough to leeward you can luff up slightly and close reach into the mark, thereby losing no speed at all.

Tactics on the second windward leg

As soon as you have started your second windward leg make sure your wind is clear and, if you are leading at this time, as soon as the second boat comes round, stay between him and the next mark. Do not let him get clear for one moment. When you are in this position the way you go up this beat depends entirely on the way the second boat goes. The chances are that he noticed which was the faster way on the first beat and will try and go that way on the second beat. He may not take into account that there is a change of tide or wind which could alter the situation. If this has happened be careful, especially of the third boat round the mark, as this is the skipper who is most likely to split off and go the way you would like to go.

If this situation should occur start using 'herding' tactics. I have found this to be very useful indeed when you have to cover two competitors of equal speed. You will find that at most times, and quite correctly, they split tacks and go opposite ways and it is a very difficult decision to make as to which one of these boats to cover. To overcome this, encourage both of them to go the same way. In just the same way as the sheepdog keeps his flock under control, so you do so with these two. It is quite easy to achieve; just make it easier for one of them to go one way than the other. Supposing you have rounded the leeward mark in the lead, and the next two boats come round very close together behind you. The third boat will tack immediately and if you sit hard enough on the second boat and really make a nuisance of yourself giving him all the back-wind possible, you will force this second boat to tack the same way as the third. As soon as he does this, you will of course cover, but not quite so completely, just allow him to feel that his course is the best one. It is

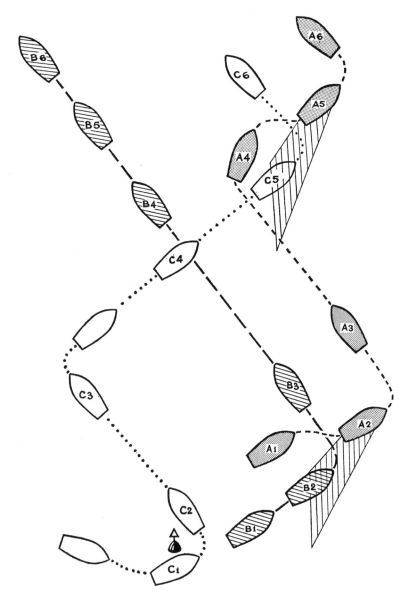

Figure 47. The principle of 'herding' tactics. The dark grey boat is in control.

then likely that the third boat will tack again and come across under the stern of the second boat. As soon as he comes within tacking range you must tack, and sit on him again, giving him plenty of back-wind and making things miserable for him. He, too, will go about again and follow the second boat and again you cover from a distance and make things easy for him. If you are clever enough you should be able to keep those two going in the same direction the whole of the distance of the windward leg. If you manage it and are doing it properly then there is little chance of either of them passing you.

If you are unlucky enough not to be in the lead round the leeward mark and you are way back around sixth or seventh, then you must try and sail the windward leg as if it was the first leg again. Work out the quickest way to the windward mark, at least you have a little help here because you know which was the fastest way on the first beat and can take this into account. There is only one snag and that is the 'X' number of boats ahead of you which you will have to pass. If you have difficulty with any individual boat I strongly recommend you try to pass him purely by speed and better tacking. If this is not feasible, then by slight adjustment of your sails you may well be able to outpoint him. If you cannot outpoint him try going a little faster and diving through his lee as it so often happens when one does this that one can romp away and end up a long way ahead but only fractionally to leeward. On the next tack it may be possible to cross their bows but a word of warning here, that if you are racing in the northern hemisphere only try and do this when you are on port tack. If you happen to be on starboard tack it is best to try and outpoint them and not go through their lee. The reason for this is, as mentioned before, the wind tends to turn clockwise during the day and if you dive down to leeward of a port tack boat and can get slightly ahead, when the wind does head you, you can go about and be up to windward of him.

At Poole in 1967, on the last beat of a race, Rodney Pattisson was two lengths ahead of us when we went round the leeward mark. The wind was playing 'silly fools' that day but it had steadied down to a direction where one could not quite lay the windward mark on port tack. After a lot of discussion in *Shadow* we decided that if the wind was going to do anything it would carry on the usual system of going clockwise, so instead of tacking to get out of Pattisson's dirty wind, or trying to outpoint him, we drove off through his lee until we were level with him but two boat lengths to leeward. Because we were clear of his dirty wind and quarter waves we managed to drive through the water just that little bit faster than him. By this time we were three-quarters of the way up the last beat and were beginning to wonder if our calculations had gone amiss, but sure enough as we were about a quarter of a mile from the finishing line the wind gradually headed just as we suspected it might. It headed enough so that when we went about on to starboard we could cross him easily and won that race by thirty seconds. Had we tried to get to the other side of him, of course, all would have been lost. Mind you, when you get ashore everybody, without exception, will say you were lucky to get that header. I agreed with them that day since I did not feel like explaining how many times this same thing had happened to me before!

Going up the second beat try and get your crew to check the length of time you spend on each tack to the windward mark. This will come in very useful on the run to help you to decide on which side you should set the spinnaker. If there was a class starting before you, you will by this time be meeting them running down on the second to last leg of their course, in which case take great care not to get anywhere near them unless you are forced to by having to cover the next boat. The amount of wind that spinnakers disturb is enormous and will go on affecting you for some time if you get among them. There will also be broken water from the quarter waves, and there may be spectator boats following this class which will also upset the wave pattern.

These running boats can be a great help to you if you are lying in second position, and being covered closely by the leading boat. If this is so, seriously consider diving in amongst this fleet so that you get him tied up with them! The idea being that if he is tacking on you closely, wait until he gets one of these running boats just slightly up to windward and then go about and he will not be able to follow for some minutes. It will at least break his cover and may give you a chance to catch up with him. This is very easy if you are second boat because you are the one who is calling the tune. Most leading boats when they get into this position get into a flap and slow themselves down even more. If the leading boat keeps cool he will know it will

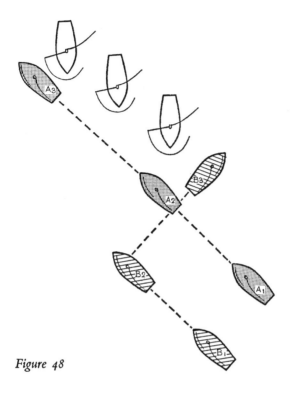

Figure 48

make little difference if he goes on a few more feet and then tacks but if you are the second boat you have to try everything to get him to break cover. If, when you get to the windward mark, you are leading be careful that the second boat does not force you to cover too early so that you cannot make the mark, otherwise you will have to put in one extra short tack which will kill your speed and allow him to catch up. The thing is to keep your weather eye on him, but bear in mind that you are in the vicinity of the windward mark and the first point is to round it as quickly as you can. This should be done with as few tacks as possible.

Starting the dead run

Quite often at this stage (again if you are leading boat) you can tack on your opponent when he has tacked and thinks that he can lay

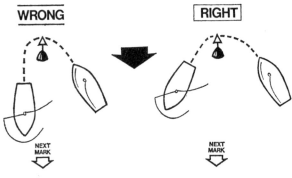

Figure 49

the windward mark. You may well have overstood it yourself, but if you free off slightly and romp, your back-wind will stop him pointing as high and you will force him either to go to leeward of the mark or put in an extra tack. Although you have overstood the mark you are reaching and in actual fact would have gained in distance over your competitor. When rounding this windward mark be careful you do not bear away hard on to a dead run straight away. This movement I have always found very critical; whenever possible one should bear away on a smooth gentle circle to keep maximum speed at all times. The chances are that before you have lost way you can get your spinnaker up and hold that speed for some while.

24. Running and the Final Beat

Spinnaker—tactics—trim—balance—leeward mark—windshifts—last wind-ward leg—windshifts—finishing line

If the wind has stayed in the same direction then this will be the first and only leg of the course with the wind aft and it is not the time to light cigarettes or relax! More distance can be won or lost on the run than any other point of sailing. On rounding that windward mark one cannot be too quick in hoisting the spinnaker. Get it up and pulling as fast as you can, but try not to set it on a dead run because it will take much longer to fill. It is better, if it is possible, to keep the wind at twenty degrees over the weather quarter. This will enable you to keep up maximum speed while it is set and it will pull much more efficiently. If you are in a dinghy, the centreboard should be nearly right up and, if you have shroud levers, let them go completely.

If you are in a keel boat try and rake the mast over the bow. I have not yet worked out why, but it is a definite advantage to let the mast go forward. There are various ways of doing this, it does not matter how, as long as they work efficiently and you can tighten up the shrouds again later.

Cunningham holes should be let off, outhauls should be slackened and the kicking strap should not be too tight, especially in medium to light winds. When the spinnaker is set and you have settled down the next problem will be on which side the spinnaker should be set. This is where your crew can help from his timing of the length of tacks from the last windward leg. If the total time for the starboard tack is greater than the total time for the port tack, then you should be on port tack on the run. Though this may not necessarily be the case if, for example, there is a strong cross current pushing you one way or the other.

The trim of the boat is most important, this should not be neglected for a minute. The fore-and-aft trim must be adjusted at all times as you go up and down a wave, and in a calm once you have found the best place, the fore-and-aft position must be stationary. There is one practice that really does make you go fast off the wind and that is for the crew and the helmsman to sit out as hard as they can on opposite sides. This also works in keel boats. Once again, I can only guess at the reason for this, I think when you sit in this position you are acting as wing ballast and in the same way as I described earlier when going to windward, you have to keep the top of the mast as still as possible. This has the same effect on the runs, the boat that is rolling all over the place does not go quite as fast as the one that is held still. This is very apparent if you have a spinnaker up as every time the boat rolls it disappears behind the mainsail and only half its area will be pulling. This practice of sitting out on the run is an everyday occurrence in the National classes of Great Britain but it does not seem to have 'caught on' internationally. Perhaps it is because they are under the illusion that the runs are for resting!

On this leg of the course the tiller must be moved only the smallest amount and a useful tip too is to try and sit on the tiller extension. This will slow down the movement of the rudder, thereby reducing the braking effect. The only time one can safely sail on a run with the wind dead astern is when it is blowing very hard and you are reaching your maximum speed. In all other conditions one must have the wind slightly on the windward quarter. The amount depends on the type of boat of course. If you do sail this way you will have to tack downwind. This is not such a great loss as it may seem, because if you are good at gybing with the spinnaker then there is no need for it to collapse at all. You must take into account wind changes just as much as on the beat, in other words if you are sailing directly to the leeward mark with the wind on the quarter all well and good, but if the wind suddenly comes round to dead astern you will have to luff up. If it goes even further round then you must gybe—and in gybing you will find that you are back on your original course with the wind on the other quarter. In other words, one has to sail the shortest possible course keeping the wind on the quarter the whole time. (See Figure 50).

Plate 54. It is good to keep the spinnaker right on the verge of luffing but this spinnaker has gone a little too far and is not pulling at its best. However, the jib fairleads are in the right place since the flow curve is exactly parallel along the jib luff.

This photograph shows how important it is to sheet the spinnaker as far aft as possible. It is not often that you can see a spinnaker from this angle and it shows how far you can get the leach of the spinnaker away from the back of the mainsail by putting the fairlead right aft. With the lead further forward the slot would have closed and the mainsail would have to be sheeted in further. Also note that the spinnaker halyard has not been pulled right up and the head of the spinnaker is at least twelve inches away from the mast, which allows the spinnaker to move forward into clear air.

Sports Illust

Plate 55. Here the spinnaker is set with the jib rolled up, which is a great advantage in very light airs so that the spinnaker can catch all the wind that is going. If there is sufficient wind then the jib can be unrolled.

A good view of the slot between the leach of the spinnaker and the mainsail. Here the sheet is led aft via a hook under the boom which pulls it more outboard allowing the leach of the spinnaker to go even further off to leeward giving greater driving power. Again note that the head of the spinnaker is well away from the mast.

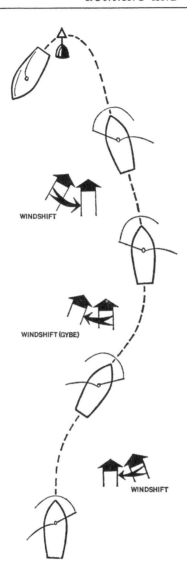

Figure 50

WINDSHIFT

WINDSHIFT (GYBE)

WINDSHIFT

Tactics when running

Covering tactics are the next thing to be taken into consideration. The first basic requirement is never to let your opponent get dead to windward of you. This is essential with a spinnaker set, but even if the class does not have a spinnaker it is just as important, since the area of a mainsail can have a devastating effect on a boat a hundred feet to leeward of it. Attacking and defending tactics on the down-wind leg are very similar to those used up wind. You should always keep between your opponents and the next mark. If your opponent goes off on the starboard gybe then you must do this as well. Making sure that you do not get in his wind shadow and that you do not gybe until you have seen that his spinnaker pole has changed from one side to the other.

He may do a dummy gybe, that is, change his main boom over from one side to the other but keeping his spinnaker exactly the same. It will stay filled efficiently even though the boom is out to leeward. You may want to cover him quickly and be so absorbed with gybing efficiently on to the new tack you do not realise what he is up to, and when you look up again you will find that having pushed his boom back again to the original side he is passing across your stern the opposite way. You must therefore keep your eyes open for such dummy gybes!

If you happen to be unfortunate enough to have rounded the windward mark way back in the fleet, this is the best opportunity you will get to catch up with the leaders. Do not follow them, at this stage, go off on either one side or the other. You will have to work out carefully which is the best side and having done so go for it. Do not be too cautious, the only way you are likely to catch up with the leaders is to go the whole way. Keep the wind on your quarter, and go as fast as you can until you estimate that by gybing and bringing the wind back on the other quarter you can lay the next mark. I do not guarantee that this will work every time but it should produce some dramatic position change! It may even put you in touch with the leaders for the final beat.

If you have a chance during the final stages of this leg try to feed yourselves plenty of liquid and instant energy, because if you thought the race was hard up to this stage then it is going to be murder on the last beat! You will need every ounce of strength to drive yourselves to the finishing line.

Approaching the lee mark

As you reach the halfway mark of this downwind leg try and work out in your mind the number of gybes you are going to make on the rest of the leg. Your main worry is that the final run into the leeward mark should be on the gybe where you can lower your spinnaker and round the mark without gybing. If you have to leave the mark to port, you should come into the mark on the port gybe and if it is a starboard hand mark then try and come in on the starboard gybe. This will save much time and avoid unnecessary risk of a snarl-up, and you will find you are able to round the mark very close indeed, so stopping anybody close astern getting up on your windward quarter.

Before you take your spinnaker down do not forget to make sure that the mast is put back to the normal position and that the outhaul is tensioned and the cunningham hole is tight and everything ready for action on the next leg.

Immediately on rounding this mark make a quick check that there are no spinnaker sheets hanging over the side and that the spinnaker halyard is not flapping in the slot of the jib or round the back of the mainsail and that everything is setting perfectly.

The last leg

Now is the time to put every ounce of effort into sailing the boat, whether or not you are a long way in the lead does not matter. So many things can happen on the last beat that never seem to happen at any other time throughout the rest of the course! I have come to the conclusion that it is because crews vary so much; some can put in a much greater amount of effort for this last leg, than others. Anyway be prepared! Forget about the right way to go on this beat, you are not at all interested, because the thing that matters now is covering those boats behind you. You can either cover the individual or you can start 'herding', but keep an eye on them all. If there happens to be a heading shift while you are covering someone, do not tack until he does. If you tack too soon you will find that he ends up windward boat.

If there is a class which started before yours nearing the finishing mark, now is the time to keep an eye on them. If you happen to see the tail enders get a freeing windshift do not wait for it—tack immediately. You must get into it before anybody else, otherwise the fourth and fifth boats dead astern of you will be able to point up and could, in theory, if it is a violent windshift, get ahead. Therefore, there are two golden rules—if a header is coming sail into it and do not tack until the others do—and if you see a freer coming do not wait until it hits you—tack for it.

If you find one person is going a little faster than you and there is nothing you can do about it you might try other means of stopping him. In the Southern area Soling championship which was held at Poole in 1969, we managed to get a good start and we were in the lead, but a 'lady helmsman' was gradually creeping up on our weather quarter. We had to tack for the mark and this other boat tacked immediately and was just under our lee, clear of our back-wind. Unfortunately, this boat was going faster than we were and after five minutes or so would have been a considerable way ahead. This called for drastic action! I said to my crew, 'Talk to her. Say something nice to her.' My crew with great presence of mind leant over and hailed her: 'Oh—— what a nice bottom you have' (she was sitting out hard). Appreciating this she laughed and waved, and as she was distracted and her concentration was broken, her boat slowed! She dropped back into our back-wind which slowed her down and she then dropped back into somebody elses', and eventually had to put in two tacks! By the time we reached the mark we could not see her number! From this it is obvious that if you can get in a 'groove' you will go very fast, but if this concentration can be broken it will take a long time to settle down again. You must guard against losing your own powers of concentration while you are wrecking their's though!

If you happen to be in second position close to and dead astern of the leader a good tactic, if he starts looking back at you at regular intervals, is to point your boat very high as he turns round. He will think you are pointing much higher than he is and will also wind up and try to point. You can bear away the minute his back is turned, but he will go on pinching which will slow him down drastically. If you then go about he will tack to cover and this will slow him down more. By this time he may even be losing his temper which is just what you want!

Approaching the finish

Races are won and lost on the finishing line. So many people make the mistake of going to the wrong end of the line, and indeed it is difficult to tell which end is the right one, that is, the nearest one to you. There are two ways of deciding this, one is by timing the tacks as you come up the last beat, so that if the total time spent on the starboard tack is more than the total time spent on the port tack then the correct end of the line (presuming it is at right angles to the last mark) is the port end. If the total time on the port tack was the greatest then the end of the line you should make for is the starboard end.

The second way of deciding is the easier, but can only be done as you are nearing the finishing line. You simply finish at the opposite end to that you would choose if you were starting. Therefore if you are pointing up high on starboard across the finishing line you will not go to the starboard end to finish but will go instead to the port end.

Having decided on the end of the line where you are going to finish and if you are in the lead, do not under any circumstances overstand. If you do this it may be possible for your opponents to come up and tack under your lee bow and scrape in between you and the distance mark. Always try not to leave any room here.

As in athletic events, do not stop once you are over the finishing line, sail on hard until you are sure you are well past it. Many times I have seen a race lost because a helmsman thought he was over the line and let everything go, and the second boat sailed on to win. I know these sound like trifling points but after a long hard race when you are tired these things can and do happen.

25. After Finishing

Unwinding—reviewing any carelessness—putting away boat—declarations —points—logging all details—analysis of race—prizes, speeches, etc.

Your work is not finished once you have reached the finishing line, you must still keep clear of all the other boats finishing until you have cleared the line. Most sailing instructions say that anybody hindering boats finishing will be disqualified. On the other hand, try not to get too far away, it can be very interesting to stay a while and see how the others cross that line. You will be able to see if you did choose the right end to finish, and sometimes if boats are finishing very close together it can be very exciting and you can learn a lot too. It will give you an idea of your points position, just a rough one as, of course, there may still be protests and retirements after the race.

If it is blowing very hard guard against carelessness. Once you are across the line you will all relax and this is when trouble usually occurs; it so often happens that boats go round the course without capsizing only to do so the minute that they have finished! If the wind is very strong roll up your jib or lower it and, if you are fortunate enough to be to windward of your base, run home under bare poles! We did this in Bendor when the wind was a steady thirty-two knots, and Rodney Pattisson, who finished just behind us, followed suit. You would be surprised at how exhilarating it can be to plane under bare poles! As far as I remember we were the only two boats to get home without capsizing that day. Although Ben Verhagen, who is a great heavy weather sailor managed to get back to base without lowering his mainsail! In fact he couldn't! He had to keep it up because he used one of the external hook-ups which, in that strength of wind made it impossible to lower the mainsail. To see him haring off down wind was a sight I shall not forget! He had capsized twice during the race.

During a good race the tension can mount up and it takes quite a while afterwards to 'unwind'. Relax and finish off your food and drink on the way home, and if possible wait for other boats to sail home in company. I find the most difficult time for unwinding is when there is very little wind and it takes a long time to get back, the noise of the sails slatting away as the boat rolls with the swell can be very tedious. Of course, the answer is to 'hitch a tow' home if you can.

Arriving back at the moorings or the shore, which ever the case may be, make sure that you unrig the boat with the utmost care. First check the position of your jib fairleads, outhaul, cunningham hole and shroud tensions, etc., so that you can note this in your log when you return to your hotel. Remove the sails from the spars and, if dry, fold them carefully, not too tight or you will get creasing, and try and fold them in a different place each day.

Spinnakers should be bundled in the sailbag until you get ashore where you can wash and dry them, and the boat should be made generally shipshape. Make a careful check of all the fittings, shroud plates, clevis pins, shackles and rope to make sure nothing has come loose, chafed or started to break. Do not forget that you have had heavy strain on these items so now is the time to see if they will stand up to the next race—if not, replace them. But, do this now. If you leave it until the next day it may be forgotten.

If it is possible, wash the boat down. It really does demoralise the opposition to come ashore and see the first boat already washed and stowed away! If the day is warm and sunny it is a good idea to leave the cover off for an hour or so and, with luck, the moisture you have soaked up during the race will dry up.

You must not forget to return your tally and sign your declaration as soon as you get ashore, before you have time to forget. I think declarations are unnecessary and pretty useless so it is a pity the whole system cannot be scrubbed.

When you have finished with the boat and have changed, check up on the points situation. At the beginning of the week it will just be a matter of interest but for the last two races it is vital that you should know who your nearest competitor is. You never know, you may meet him in the bar that evening and if you work on him you may get him in the right frame of mind to finish behind you in the next race!

The value of keeping a log

Enter all the details in your log-book that evening; include an analysis of the race, with the additional information on the speed of the other boats and the wind strength and sea conditions. If possible you should put down the reasons you think these boats were performing in this way in those particular conditions. Be very self-critical, if you think you are not tacking fast enough put it down—if you think one of the crew is talking too much enter that too (and make sure he reads it)! In this way mistakes can be rectified before the next race. If it happened to be the last race and you have won, still carry out these procedures, as there will always be other races and what you noticed today may help you win tomorrow! (See Appendix)

I do think, that if you have won a prize you must make every effort to get to the prizegiving. It is a bit tough on the organizers who have worked very hard over a long period to make the week a success if half the competitors are not there to receive the trophies.

Speeches, unfortunately, there will always be. If you are like me and hopeless at the job make it short and sweet, for the sake of those who are forced to listen! When I was sailing National Twelves it was my burning ambition to win the Points Cup, I had won the Burton Trophy and come within half a point of the Points several times, so when I did finally make it at Falmouth, my crew could just not understand why it was that the minute we crossed the finishing line I was reduced to quiet misery, instead of leaping around the boat with excitement! It was the horrible thought that I had to make a speech! It quite ruined the rest of the day for me!

If you are many miles from home and have to catch a Channel ferry back try and organise your travelling to allow you to stay the last night in the hotel, and start off fresh the following day. In fact, organise the whole journey in the same way that you managed the outward trip.

If you are returning with silverware do not forget to declare it through Customs. I have never had any trouble and, as long as you can assure them that the trophies were won in International competition they seem quite happy.

I think the most difficult thing about international sailing is trying to reacclimatise yourself when you return home to the Saturday club race. What was once so important, now seems a little dull, and you will find that in no time at all you are planning another jaunt to the bigger and better regattas!

Appendices

CHECK LIST BEFORE SAILING

Check that:

The underside of boat is clean
No stones are in the centreboard case
The rigging is satisfactory
All clevis pins, split pins, links are in place
Spinnaker is dry
You have signed out
You have read the weather forecast
You know the time of high and low water
There is nothing important on the official notice board

Check that the following items are in the boat:

food and water
a stopwatch
a spinnaker boom
boom
battens
rudder
tiller
bungs
sailing instructions
trapeze belt
protest flag
ensign
means of bailing
tools (pliers, screwdriver,
   knife)
spare sails
spare clothing
paddle
compasses
jib sheets

mainsheet
spinnaker sheet
winch handles
jib
mainsail
spinnaker
spinnaker turtle
aspirin
sun-glasses
burgee
tally
anchor and warp
binoculars
oilskins
gloves
spare shackles
chinagraph pencil
chart of the course
first aid kit

PRACTICE OUT ON COURSE:

Sail hard to windward
Tacking
Gybing with and without spinnaker
Rounding marks

Spinnaker hoisting
Spinnaker lowering
Spinnaker reaching
Running
Starting

AFTER THE FIRST DAY'S SAILING CHECK BOAT AND CARRY
OUT ANY REPAIRS NECESSARY

CHECK LIST BEFORE STARTING

Make boat shipshape
Check spinnaker sheets are clear
Check when sailing out to start for wind-bends and/or permanent shifts
Check tacking angle and reduce if possible
Check if wind in the gusts is heading or freeing you
Keep near starting line (in light winds keep up-tide of line)

Thirty minutes before start:

Eat and drink
Check outhaul and cunningham tensions
Check centreboard and rudder for weed
Remove all water from inside of boat
Pass spare sails and clothing over to friends
Check everything in boat is in place
Check compass bearing of windward mark and note it down
Check direction and strength of tide
Check wind direction and windshift pattern
Check which end of line is best
Check bearing of line (each way, and note it down)
Check if committee's windward mark bearing is the same as yours!
If class starting ahead of you, check their guns for discrepancy in starters'
    watch
Get near committee boat in time for ten-minute gun

Ten minutes

Check boat is in tune for existing conditions
Check rudder and centreboard for weed
Take glucose for instant energy
Get back near the committee boat for five minute gun

Five minutes

Check gun for discrepancy in timing
Keep clear of other boats
Check if 5-, 2- or 1-Minute Rule is in operation
Crew to count down (every 10–20 seconds—not too loud!)
Keep near the line

Two minutes to go

Keep near the line

One minute to go

At this time you should be in position for starting

START
Do not pinch, try and sail fast
Ease out sheets
Keep your wind clear

CHECK LIST TO TAKE PART IN A REGATTA ABROAD

Join the A.A. or R.A.C.
Book ferry tickets
Purchase maps of the route
Passports or visa—O.K.?
International driving licence
Carnet for boat and trailer
Insurance—Car (green card)—Medical—Personal baggage
Book accommodation
Send entry form and copy of certificate
Obtain spare trailer wheel and bearings and grease gun
Arrange for currency and traveller's cheques
Chart of the area in which you are going to race
A land map of the area which shows hills
A tidal chart and tide tables
Met. records for the area for the time of year of the regatta
Obtain sailing instruction as soon as possible
Dry sails in airing cupboard (two weeks before leaving)
Fit a bottom as well as a top cover
Have car serviced a few weeks before leaving
Check all trailer lights and headlight reflectors
Check boat measurements before leaving
Food and liquid for the journey
Mark position of shrouds, mast, sheet leads, etc., before unrigging the boat
On arrival at destination

Check into hotel
Report at regatta office
Obtain the best berth (get keel boats afloat now)
Unpack boat
Step mast
Check mast tenon is a tight fit
Find out your time for measuring

Check boat when fully rigged to see if anything is missing
Learn sailing instructions by heart
Sail out on the course
Check tide against tide chart
Check for wind-bends over the course
Check if wind direction has changed during the day
On returning, cover the boat up before it dries out
Analyse your findings for the day
Get the boat ready for measuring
Measure boat—measure sails
Paint black bands on spars (check by measurer)
Re-rig boat as soon as possible

LOG FOR RACE AT: ON:

BOAT: NO. OF STARTERS: FINISHING POSITION:

RACE: DISTANCE: DURATION: STATE OF TIDE:

WEATHER: Wind strength: Sea State:
         Wind direction: Sea Temp: Air Temp:

WINDSHIFTS NOTED:

PERFORMANCE: At the start: At the finish:
             On the wind: On the reach:
             Sail handling: On the run:

SAILS: Main: Jib: Spi:

LIST OF ADJUSTMENTS, TENSIONS AND SETTINGS:
Main halyard	Mast heel	Which battens?
Jib halyard	Mast bend	Top batten
Spi halyard	Backstay	Main traveller
Jib Cunningham	Forestay	Sheet tension
Main Cunningham	Upper stays	Centreboard angle
Jib fairleads	Lower stays	Rudder blade angle
Jib sheets	Jumpers	Fore and aft trim
Mainsail clew	Spreader angle	All-up crew weight
Boom vang	Spreader length	

CREW and
WEIGHTS: 1.   2.   3.

FOOD AND WATER CONSUMED:

WHAT WENT WRONG?

REPAIRS OR MODIFICATIONS NEEDED:

PERFORMANCE OF LEADING COMPETITORS: